AUTHENTIC LEADERSHIP

AUTHENTIC LEADERSHIP

Embracing Your Archetypal Gifts

Angie McCourt

Disclaimer - This book does not replace the advice of a medical professional. Consult your physician before making any changes to your diet or regular health plan. To maintain the anonymity of the individuals involved, I have changed some details. The information in this book was correct at the time of publication, but the author does not assume any liability for loss or damage caused by errors or omissions. These are my memories, from my perspective, and I have tried to represent events as faithfully as possible. I've also included statements from interviews conducted in research for this book. Those commentaries are documented with the contributor's name. Some sample scenarios in this book are fictitious. Any similarity to actual persons, living or dead, is coincidental.

Authentic Leadership: Embracing Your Archetypal Gifts
Copyright © 2022 Angie McCourt
Second book in the series.
All rights reserved. No part of this book may be reproduced or used in any manner without prior written permission of the copyright owner, except for the use of brief quotations in a book review.

To request permission, contact the publisher at angie@angiemccourt.com.

Paperback ISBN: 978-1-7376831-3-1
eBook - Kindle ISBN: 978-1-7376831-4-8
Library of Congress Control Number: 2022917451

First paperback edition October 2022

Cover art by Lauren Diamond
Photography by Shawna Benson Photography

Published by Authentic Me Revolution LLC

www.angiemccourt.com/loveyourgifts

DEDICATION

This book is dedicated to all the authentic leaders I've had the pleasure of working with and witnessing over the years. Those who helped me shape my own leadership style, those who modeled authentic leadership when it was needed most and those currently on their own authentic leadership journey. I appreciate the many who contributed to this book to allow for validation of the leadership evolution and the opportunity to capture real-time transformation. I've enjoyed witnessing their leadership journeys over the years whether they led people or initiatives.

DEDICATION

Our authenticity is our superpower.
— Jamie Kern Lima

CONTENTS

PART ONE BEHAVIOR PATTERNS OF OUTDATED LEADERSHIP STYLES 1
- DESPERATE FOR EMPATHY 3
- LACK OF PRESENCE 9
- DANG ASSUMPTIONS 15
- COMMAND AND CONTROL IS OUTDATED 21
- FALSE CELEBRITY STATUS 27
- NOT FEELING VALUED 33
- HIERCHICAL MINDSET BREAKDOWN 39
- FEAR OF FAILURE IMPACTS 45
- SELF-IMPOSED DECISION FATIGUE 51
- SELF PRESERVATION BEHAVIORS 57
- JUDGMENT OF EXPRESSION 63

PART TWO EVOLVED AUTHENTIC LEADERSHIP GIFTS 71
- EMPATHIC CAPACITY 73
- ALL FORMS OF INNOVATION 77
- INITIATIVE IS THE SPARK 81
- CRAVING ACKNOWLEDGMENT 85
- SEEING THE BEST IN OTHERS 89
- ALIGNMENT IS KEY 93
- BE THE BRIDGE 97
- SUPER SUPPORTING ROLE 101
- NEEDING AN AMBASSADOR 105
- INCLUSION WINS EVERY TIME 109
- BUILDING FOUNDATIONS 113

PART THREE INTEGRATING YOUR AUTHENTIC LEADERSHIP GIFTS 117

QUALITIES FOR BALANCE... 119
CREATE SAFE SPACE... 123
OVERCOME JUDGMENT OF EXPRESSION..................................... 127
INVEST IN CONNECTIONS... 131
EMPOWERED INNOVATION 135
NURTURING LEADERSHIP... 137
CHAMPIONING PEOPLE... 141
FINDING AUTHENTIC LEADERSHIP.. 145
MY LEADERSHIP JOURNEY.. 149
YOUR AUTHENTIC LEADERSHIP 153
THE EVOLUTION.. 157

PREFACE

Authentic leadership is a passion of mine. Over the years I've found that leadership styles and principles evolve especially as we take on new roles, lead in new environments and the needs of teams change. My view of leadership and being a leader does not mean that you are managing people. It means that you are driving innovation, progress, and outcomes.

Anyone can do that, and I believe the opportunity for more leaders to bloom is on the horizon. More folks will break through inner and glass ceilings to find their purpose and meaningful work within their environment, just in a different way. Companies and leaders supporting this evolution will be the ones who are driving sustainable and differentiated companies.

I think about the role of the Knight in chess and in history. While the knight is not the king or queen, they are responsible for outcomes. They are responsible for inspiring and strategically providing direction to get to those outcomes.

So often we forget about history and how leadership has been shaped by it. One knight that offers a great story of authentic leadership although was short-lived in real life was Joan of Arc.

"Her visions compelled her to seek an audience with the future King Charles VII, who was fighting English forces over control of the French throne when she was 17 years old. She led French armies and was at Charles' side when he was crowned in 1429. In 1430, she was thrown from her horse during a battle and eventually turned over to church officials, who charged her with witchcraft, heresy, and dressing as a man. In 1431, at 19 years old, she was burned at the stake.[1]

She created military strategies, wore a suit of armor, and tied her armies' victories in battle to her religious faith. Like many knights, she also won a title for herself and her descendants through her brave deeds: King Charles VII granted her family arms and nobility. Joan of Arc has long been a national hero of France. She was canonized as a saint in 1920."

In the olden days, knights were considered one of the most trustworthy and appropriate for a mission. Therefore, knights are often referred to as "knights in shining armor". The fact that a knight uniquely attacks by jumping over opponents is also in line with the old saying that says knights "get by on guts, not gadgets." When you have a struggle in life and you begin to play out how you will resolve it, you are utilizing your inner knight.

The knight in chess is important because it moves differently than any other chess piece. Above all, the knight in chess is very powerful. The knight represents the pure inner warrior. It can't move very far, but it never moves in a straight line, always preferring to be tactical and thoughtful. The knight is one of the most difficult pieces to learn how to play, but it is also one of the most valuable pieces in the endgame.

Authentic leadership also provides this type of value in business and for companies to navigate change and uncertainty. Ensuring it is a strategic approach will be a game changer for your business and teams. Developing your own authentic leadership is a capacity that will help you stand out not only to the teams or initiatives you lead, but to the results you will be able to achieve with consistency and sustainability.[2]

---

[1] Gershon, Livia. "Eight Knights Who Changed History" *History*. August 26, 2019, https://www.history.com/news/knights-middle-ages
[2] "What Chess Pieces Represent (Meaning & Symbolism" *MrsCheckmate*. https://www.mrscheckmate.com/what-chess-pieces-represent/

INTRODUCTION

Many times, throughout history there have been major shifts in leadership evolution. The last major shift in leadership evolution started in the 1990's which is when leadership as a unidirectional, top-down influencing process where a distinct line was drawn between leaders and followers. Instead, the focus became on the complex interactions among the leader, the followers, the situation, and the system as a whole through transactional and transformational leadership theories. Transformational leadership is a theory in which leaders encourage, inspire, and motivate followers. Examples of transformational leaders during this time include the likes of Jeff Bezos, Steve Jobs and Bill Gates. Transactional leadership relies on authority to motivate colleagues. The rapid change, disruptive technological innovation and increasing globalization created a need for this leadership evolution.

Here we are again on the precipice of leadership evolution because what used to work doesn't work anymore. For instance, where we could predict what's going to happen next quarter, next month, next year started to become challenging even before COVID, it was very hard for us to even forecast as a company and a business. The feeling when we don't have control over this anymore is because we were only ever working with this old system and structure of how we set goals and how we monitored them. The decisions that we made along the way or didn't make along the way to be more agile in our approach were tough to practice. To make shifts and to change direction as we needed was always reactive.

As we continue to face uncertainty, unpredictability, non-linear speed of change and in a virtual world along with structures and massive boundary spanning we need a new way to lead business and people. I believe this evolution is also sparked by people. People's need to be seen and treated as human, to contribute in a greater way than work has been defined in the past and on their terms. What is required of leaders in this new theory? If you listen closely, you'll hear all the answers you need. In the meantime, I'll outline them as succinctly as possible.

They want authenticity, connection, collaboration, cooperation, flow, adaptability, flexibility, freedom, communication, trust, autonomy, empowerment and enablement, clarity, transparency, and alignment. Without force, control, micromanagement, ambiguity, shame, and fear. Sounds simple right? I view this evolution as one of the most challenging we have seen. This evolution is such a shift from previous styles and practices that it will take a lot of introspection, connection, vulnerability, and practicality to allow for it to form. I call this the age of authentic leadership.

> *"Leaders are human too"*
> ——Rach A

What is authentic leadership? Authentic root is 'you are the author of your destiny'. The word leader has an older pedigree – from the Old English lædere, "one who leads", agent noun from lædan, "to guide, bring forth" Travel internally (self-discovery). The closest word in antiquity relating to leadership is the Latin word ducere "to lead, consider, regard" according to Etymologeek.[3]

---

[3] https://etymologeek.com/search/all/leader

The term has so many meanings: direction, guidance, transformation, facilitation, orchestration, servitude and more. All in all, leadership is based on our belief system. Authentic leadership is our belief in our destiny to guide others or to create.

Here is what Janee Francks shared in our conversation on leadership style. "Leadership style is based on a mindset of a belief system that includes our values and principles. The new style of leadership ties into business agility and the way we work." She is so right! The opportunity in this evolution to authentic leadership is that we create the structures, systems, beliefs, and alignment that support what is needed to provide the best environment for innovation.

> *"Putting a certain leader with certain skills in place can set the tone and trajectory for an organization. If another leader would have been put in place instead that trajectory would have been different."*
> ——Nicko Roussos

Let's talk about ego. I touched on ego in my first book introduction as well and really want to dive in a bit deeper here as sometimes this can battle with authentic leadership. Linda Rendleman states "some people with false ego are very good at managing up and telling people what they want to hear to make them believe that they're excellent at managing down. That can make things painful for a team. One of the things I think leaders of leaders can do is continue to drive awareness around false ego and build awareness around the importance of authenticity."

In this book, my intention is to outline how we get to authentic leadership through identifying the 'blocks' that hold us back from igniting our authentic leadership gifts that will fulfill the requirements today. There are so many gifts that have been dormant for decades in the workplace due to the lack of value that has historically been put on them. This book is meant to showcase these gifts and their important in leadership. I also want to offer some real-life guidance on how to implement these gifts in a way that is authentic and effective.

In Part 1, I will share many of the blocks that can hold us back from authentic leadership and from unlocking the gifts that are the foundation to this evolution. I also provide Make the Shift suggestions on how to break through the blocks or enhance your power in these areas. My biggest suggestion is to be open (heart not ego) and dive into these to understand their impact and why it's important to break through them.

In Part 2, we will walk through the authentic leadership archetypal gifts that can unlock the new way of leading. I'll share outlines of the gifts, the impact they can have, the challenges that can come with them and examples of leaders who have modeled these gifts. While many of the gifts will feel more familiar in the business world, just maybe not modeled enough there are many gifts in this book that I outline that may be uncomfortable or you are new to viewing them as valuable due to their more feminine quality nature.

These include Nurturer to bring forth empathy and establish relationships in an authentic, caring, and deeper way. Visionary bringing forth a long-term vision. Advocate bringing forth acknowledgment. Clarifier creating alignment across groups, strategy, and messaging. Connector as the bridge between people and to the big picture. Champion hitting discomfort head on and servicing people. Collaborator as an authentic inclusive approach to co-creation.

In Part 3, you will read about stories of leaders who have integrated these authentic leadership gifts into their style and what it has meant for them as well as learn more about the significant need to find harmony with our masculine and feminine qualities. This is not a gender thing, it's an energy thing. All people have both qualities. It's a matter of how we utilize them to do our work and lead others in a way that is aligned and effective.

There is an opportunity to be more real-time in managing business instead of in the rears and to adjust as we flow. Goal setting can be more of an outcome instead of the only focus. Opening ourselves to look at how we ebb and flow with business instead of forcing it will offer more effective ways of connecting to customers, providing solutions that solve problems and not create more. Co-creation across teams will allow us to work within the non-linear crazy speed of change and collaboration will become a true structure for getting work done. Much of this has to do with how we use our skills, capacities, qualities, and energy.

I hope you enjoy this book and find it as a helpful guide on your journey to authentic leadership. I'm here to support you and encourage your leadership transformation.

PART ONE
BEHAVIOR PATTERNS OF OUTDATED LEADERSHIP STYLES

1
DESPERATE FOR EMPATHY

The more aligned you are with your authentic self the more resilient and adaptable you become.
—Karen Curry Parker

Apathy persists

There is a need or even desperation for empathy specifically from leaders in the workplace. Empathy as defined by Merriam-Webster [4] is "the action of understanding, being aware of, being sensitive to, and vicariously experiencing the feelings, thoughts, and experience of another of either the past or present without having the feelings, thoughts, and experience fully communicated in an objectively explicit manner". I love this definition over others as it's more complete in that showing that empathy does not mean we need to communicate to us to feel it. This offers a foundation for authentic leadership.

Levels of empathy fell by 48% between 1979 and 2009. [5]

---

[4] Merriam-Webster ttps://www.merriam-webster.com/dictionary/empathy
[5] Konrath, S.H., O'Brien, E.H., Hsing, C. "Changes in dispositional empathy in American college students over time: a meta-analysis" *Personality and Social Psychology Review*, August 2010, Advanced Online Publication. https://pubmed.ncbi.nlm.nih.gov/20688954/

When there is a lack of empathy in the workplace or in leadership it can come across as apathy, a "lack of feeling or emotion, interest, enthusiasm, or concern" according to Merriam-Webster.[6] Often this impacts our authenticity in our engagement with others.

> *"Are you real, no mask? We want to know our leaders are human."*
> ———Rach

Why does apathy happen? Often, when leaders are overwhelmed, micromanaged or under extreme pressure to deliver many of the 'softer' skills and capacities can become smaller within our leadership style. There is a sense of survival that kicks in and every person is out for themselves. Fear typically drives this disconnection as well. Disconnection from emotions, motivation, and care for others in this way.

The impact apathy has on teams can create disengagement, lack of accountability and an extension of everyone for themselves survival mode. Collaboration ceases to be effective and typically customer experience suffers due to lack of cohesiveness across teams. Robotic modes of task doing can also ignite apathy. It's all about getting the task done versus the impact this task can bring to others. Problem solving also become challenging because often solutions are half-baked and not owned for implementation and effectiveness.

Apathy then impacts the business because disjointed approaches become confusing for customers. Focus on customers becomes almost nonexistent and forward thinking shrinks back up to the day-month-quarter focus. If leaders no longer care about the customers or team members it is seen, felt and heard across the organization. Leaders lose influence.

Empathy is not only desperately needed from a sense of the alternative being unacceptable, but for the people. As we are evolving, we are seeking

---

[6] Merriam-Webster https://www.merriam-webster.com/dictionary/apathy

more meaning in our work, extending ourselves out of our comfort zone and open to stepping into our growth edges of possibility. If there is empathy for how imperfectly perfect, we attempt this expansion and evolution we feel seen and heard, not judged. There becomes a sense of sponsorship allowing the team members to be their authentic human self and bring in their best.

In working with clients, I often hear about current or past leaders who did and didn't show empathy and the impact it had on them. Past leader's small, disconnected comments had big impacts on confidence today. All business and no connection to the person made them feel like a number. The key is to understand how being an authentic leader incorporates empathy and not just in a singular way. Having cultural awareness and showing vulnerability also play into how empathy can be received.

By using observation, conversation, and intuition to tune into the emotional drivers behind behavior of team members including the joys and fears can reveal motivations for creative, professional, and even personal goals. Ultimately, this all gives the insight that helps a leader encourage and direct professional growth, but it also gives you the expanded common ground that can avoid demoralization and alienation. Feeling understood, especially by a manager or leader, is validating and builds trust and loyalty.

Linda recalls, "I've had leaders that were authentic and their ability to truly connect with their team made them extraordinary. My best example of this is Ken Lamneck, who just retired last December 2021. He got the very best out of me because he demonstrated he cared for my growth and development as a member of the team, but also for me as a person. One of the strongest memories I have of his demonstration of this was his attendance at my college graduation. I went back to school in my thirties to get my undergrad and he knew how hard I worked to give 100% to the company, raise my son, and do the work needed to graduate all at the same time. He stood in the back of the graduation where the student procession entered the ceremony so that he could look me in the eye and tell me congratulations and shake my hand. I was one of the student speakers that day, and a week later, he brought in the newspaper article that talked about my speech at the graduation to make sure that I had a copy. That's the kind of leader that he was. Little things like that are the complete difference to me between a fantastic leader that people want to follow and someone who is a cheerleader and says all the right words, but the feeling of the connectedness is just not there. This is an example of someone going the extra mile, but it doesn't always have to take this much effort. The desire to connect in a way that is authentic just has to be present"

Closed-minded
How often have you thought about being more empathic towards someone, but you don't understand or relate to their situation or decisions? There are many examples of how a closed-minded person shows up. They may block others from speaking. Lack a deep sense of humility. They don't like their ideas challenged. They rarely ask questions and instead prefer statements. Their focus is on being understood rather than to understand. They hold closely to what they believe and aren't willing to change. They have more interest in being proven right than hearing other perspectives. They have trouble having two conflicting thoughts in their head at the same time. They start off by saying, "I could be wrong, but...." To convince themselves and others they are open-minded when they are not.

When we are closed minded to people, situations, beliefs, or possibilities we detach from empathy. As we detach from empathy, we disconnect from others which causes us to stop co-creating. Then we stop influencing and somewhere in there we lose credibility. Positive motivation turns into fear-based leadership and keeps us from connecting authentically. You can reverse this scenario to expose the impacts being closed minded has on empathy. It's crazy how impactful being open minded is to our evolution and authentic leadership.

We have been conditioned to think in black or white, right or wrong, good or bad and taking one side over another. There is a happy medium I like to work with my group clients on and that is holding paradox or sit in the mystery. Think about a time when you were extremely committed to a project, yet you missed a meeting. You were all in and a mess at the same time. It's ok to be somewhere in the middle. Or you really liked an idea or solution one person shared yet you found inspiration in the other idea or solution. Holding paradox or the mystery is when we step into both the complexity and ambiguity to find a third option. It can help to discover totally new choices or solutions/ideas we did not even consider before. It allows us to do both, care for others and for ourselves.

"To be open minded, we must empathize with the viewpoints of others, and this requires the intellectual emotion of sympathy. And anyone who believes a certain idea or argument is intellectually compelling has a favorable attitude toward it that in effect amounts to mild affect or emotion. All belief therefore involves emotion, and no belief is purely intellectual or cognitive. Our rationalistic thinking about the mind and its justifications has been one sided." According to Michael Slote in his book From Enlightenment to Receptivity: Rethinking Our Values. [7]

Being open minded expands our adaptive capacities. Research suggests that people are more likely to be open-minded when they are not under time pressure (Our gut reactions aren't always the most accurate.) Individuals are more likely to be open-minded when they believe they are making an important decision. (This is when we start making lists of pros

---

[7] Slote, Michael "From Enlightenment to Receptivity: Rethinking Our Values" *Oxford University Press,* 2013.

and cons, seeking the perspectives of others, etc.) according to University of Pennsylvania. [8]

When we expand our adaptive capacities, we flow more fluidly through decision making and normally stressful conflicts. This ties back into unlocking our capacity for empathy as well.

Empathy is categorized as a critical leadership skill—one that helps you influence others in your organization, anticipate stakeholders' concerns, respond to team member needs more authentically, and even run better meetings. Though empathy is essential to leading and managing others—without it, you'll make disastrous decisions and forfeit the benefits—failing to recognize its limits can impair individual and organizational performance. It's exhausting because we use our full self— mind, body, heart to empathize. Empathy can get in the way of judgment and decision making because we are too connected to someone/thing.

Just like with everything else in life there is a balance needed. An awareness and authentic empathy that others need right now as well as accountability and sound judgment.

Make the Shift

How to find authentic empathy:
- Cultivate curiosity about others.
- Discover commonalities.
- Avoid complaining and reacting.
- Live in another's shoes. What are they going through, dealing with?
- Listen deeply and show vulnerability.
- Take a deep breath and empathize with your adversary.
- Stay balanced between empathy and authenticity.

---

[8] Team "Open-Mindedness" *University of Pennsylvania Authentic Happiness*, 2004. https://www.authentichappiness.sas.upenn.edu/newsletters/authentichappinesscoaching/open-mindedness

2

LACK OF PRESENCE

Don't shoot the messenger for revealing uncomfortable truths.
—— Julian Assange

Distraction
When there are important meetings, your team needs you to show up to, out of respect be on time and be present. That includes not multi-tasking during meetings including being on laptops and phones. Distraction is a habit. A bad one when you are supposed to be focused and present in a conversation or collaboration.

"During 1:1's I've had a leader totally not present and distracted by an issue they were tracking. I felt like it was a complete waste of my time."
——anonymous

The impact our distractions have not only on team members, speakers or customers/stakeholders you are trying to build a relationship or learn from, but on the information you are actually receiving. See here's the kicker! Our subconscious mind distorts, deletes, and generalizes the millions of bits of information we receive daily. This is a survival technique.

Now imagine you are in a meeting hearing the roll-out of a new program or objective the company is focused on, and you become distracted with your phone, email or thoughts. What was missed isn't even going to partially show up in that distorted, deleted, or generalized storage of the information. It won't even register. Our brains can only truly focus on one thing at a time.

Our thoughts can be one of the biggest distractions whether we are trying to solve a problem or thinking ahead and planning out the afternoon or checking our to-do list in our mind. Another distracting thought process is how to stay ahead in a conversation. Have you ever found yourself thinking about your answer while the other person is still talking and sharing? Yes, we all do it.

It's interesting to be a 3rd party listening to a conversation when this is happening by one or both participants. As a non-participant in the conversation, you can focus heavily on what is being said and received. You immediately see gaps, identify tangents and misinformation/interpretations happening all over the place. Try this out.

Let's talk a bit about deep listening and what that really means. Many times, we say I'm trying to improve my listening, but continue to plan responses in conversation or allow distractions to veer our attention from the conversation. Deep listening is not only listening with our ears. It includes listening with our heart, but wisdom and paying attention to non-verbal cues as well. If you are looking away from someone when they are speaking you won't even receive the non-verbal cues like body language, facial expressions, and eye cues.

Set the intention before a conversation or meeting (especially a video call) to show up fully engaged and present. Turn off distractions and give your full attention to that time and space as well as people. Check in with ways to keep yourself focused like taking notes (handwriting) and looking at the speakers.

Another approach to reducing distractions as a leader is to determine if you are even supposed to be in the meeting to begin with.

If you 'just want to listen in' I can guarantee you distraction will set in easily and you won't be present. So why spend the time and show up modeling the opposite of being present. Trust the attendees, share your inputs ahead of time or do a follow-up with an attendee to align if you feel the need to. Don't show up though.

Lastly, let's focus on how distractions can cause a lot of extra work, procrastination and missed opportunities in our day. More than likely, you have a lot on your plate, are in a fast-paced environment, have unrealistic goals or even doing multiple jobs. When our to-do list dictates our life and most of it includes things that don't excite us, we become bored. Distractions are the way our mind offsets spending time doing something we just don't want to do and leads us into procrastination.

When we don't review our priorities regularly to ensure we are putting our time and focus on what is needed in the most optimal way we can easily become distracted by lesser important or impactful tasks. Besides (re)prioritizing and staying aligned to objectives providing intention and attention can help break through distractions and get the work done more effectively and in a meaningful way.

Setting intention around a project or goal is a big key to revealing intrinsic motivation to creating a plan and taking actions to get it done. Why is this important? How can you contribute? What skills and capacities do you bring to getting it done? What is in it for you? What is in it for others? What is in it for the greater organization or good? Then with intention to giving full attention to what you are creating, planning, solving, executing, or communicating will have more meaning, ownership and accountability and you will have less distraction.

Disengaged

Presence is when we show up fully in our authentic skin (mind, body, heart) ready to listen, engage and/or act. Presence is becoming such a skill to be able to do this without the increasing number of distractions. When we show up in body or mind only, we can come across as disengaged. Being fully present is when we set everything else aside and make the decision to show up fully.

This isn't an easy thing to do. Many times, we can come across as being disengaged. This can happen in intimate conversations or team settings, but it can also happen when the leader is not aware of what is happening with the team. This can happen in two ways.

Feedback from contributors on disengagement. "When there is a lack of awareness of what is going on with the team the leader seems disengaged. When the leader becomes all about the business, they forget their main role as coach/developer of people and don't have conversations about career and growth."

A disengaged leader also ignores the issues going on within the team, organization or cross-departmentally it can cause a significant disconnect from what the leader is trying to push (to achieve) and how or if the team members are able to do it. This can frustrate team members because it looks like the leaders doesn't have a clue and may even commit them to unrealistic expectations that end up making the team fail or look bad. This can include bad processes, unclear policies, mis-aligned strategy, or lack of support from other groups.

Continued feedback, "when I have to follow-up with a leader to get support or answers I feel like I am not important, and that the leader is disengaged. Now I do realize they may be busy, but if they offered support or answers and then don't follow-through they are disengaged."

Let's say you work with someone you don't particularly like. You may not like how they act like a know-it-all or are trying to control a conversation, or you simply don't trust them. When they speak you tend to look away, write a note or grab your phone. Immediately you disengage. It's almost automatic no matter how much they may be growing and improving. It's a big deal to work through the dislike.

People are craving connection now more than any time in our history. As authentic leadership evolves to embrace this human desire empathy will play a role in this connection. There are many wounds being exposed of not feeling heard or seen and the worst thing we can do as leaders is to come across as disengaged. When a leader shows up disengaged today it's even more impactful than just a few years ago. Colleagues are not putting up with it. They are calling out the b.s.

Authentic leadership is about connection and doing what you say you're going to do. It's about focusing on the team member, giving them space, and amplifying their gifts while coaching them into their growth edges. The most engaged and present leader will be the one who takes this new requirement of leadership and establishes it naturally.

There is such a balance to the ebb and flow between managing the business and the people. Authentic leaders have structures in place that allow for this balance to seem natural including scheduled 1:1's, team meetings, skip level meetings and regular engagements with peers. They also have feedback loops and expectations for updates in a proactive way. Showing interest in what the team is doing and what the leader can help support goes a long way.

Make the Shift

Create a discipline to be fully present (in and out of the office)
1. Slow down your thoughts. Allow thoughts to float by without grabbing them.
2. Tap into your senses: Listen, See, Smell, Taste, Feel. Close your eyes and run through your senses.
3. Listen deeply including your heart, gut, and mind. Observe non-verbal cues.

4. Connect your mind, body, heart, wisdom into your attention and intention for showing up.

3

DANG ASSUMPTIONS

Trade expectation for appreciation and your whole world changes in an instant
——Tony Robbins

False Expectations
Assumptions are like a four-letter word to me. I've found them useful sometimes in making decisions where I may not have all the information or in profit modeling, but not in day to day at all. When there is an opportunity to seek clarity, do it. Today, count how many assumptions you make. Then do another check tomorrow or end of week to see how many were incorrect and possibly caused frustration or damage.

There is a reason when we make assumptions, we feel more stressed. It's unnecessary stress often because we are afraid to seek feedback or working too fast to think about it. They can cause a waste of time and energy. We can put energy into believing assumptions for years before challenging them. This can also cause us to miss taking opportunities.

Let's use the example of starting a new job or gaining a new boss. We assume they expect us to get something done tonight that they talked about today. We stay up until 1:00 in the morning, wake up exhausted only to find that this wasn't what was expected. Another time we assume that someone is mad at us because they canceled a meeting and are avoiding us. Finally, they share (we didn't ask ugh) they were dealing with some family issues and were refocused.

How about that time we were feeling pressured to solve a problem and that it fell on our shoulders. We didn't ask for help because we thought the expert on this was too busy and we didn't want to bother them. Instead, we solved it, and it didn't work. Many times, we create more obstacles for ourselves when we make assumptions.

You might be asking how do I break this cycle of assumptions. This is where it is so important to be aware of expectations. Often, we work under false expectations because we are assuming something instead of seeking clarity. Recognizing expectations, we have on ourselves, or others will offer a big opportunity to challenge their truth.

Once I was leading an initiative in my company that had some guidance by a consulting company. The goals that we set as part of the initiative were aggressive which wasn't an issue for me or my team. We were ready to take on the challenge. The issue was that the areas of focus were unrealistically aggressive. Since most senior leaders were not aware of the processes within teams or deliverables to customers, they didn't challenge the assumptions being made in the data and cost savings by the consulting company. It looked great and they believed the false expectations. Then the work to make it happen was left to my team.

Not only did we take on that work, but to achieve the high-level cost savings expectations we needed to go find additional areas of focus to gain it from. Of course, the consulting company was no longer in the picture during this time. The false expectations made it extremely difficult to achieve and even harder to break through disappointment and educate so we wouldn't go down this path again.

Working against false expectations is extremely exhausting, distracting and demotivating. In the end, false expectations almost always result in disappointment. Of course, this can happen with our own expectations of how something is going to happen, how we are going to contribute to or benefit from as well. When we set a goal and attach to false expectations of how it will happen, we can prevent achievement of the goal. Setting false expectations of others is one of the biggest disappointments set ups. Releasing our expectations of others and aligning with their abilities and capabilities is important. Even more important is communicating our expectations in a very clear and direct manner so they receive and understand.

When someone else has false expectations of us it can lead to extra work, stress and missed objectives. It's so important that we seek clarity and are transparent about what we can/cannot control and what we believe is doable. This doesn't mean to sandbag on every commitment. It means to commit in a way that offers credibility, stretch and a thought-out plan to achieve.

Unclear Communication

I've seen really motivating communication, clear and direct communication, and ambiguous communication from leaders. What is interesting is often it comes down to the information the leader has and how they want to distill it down into a valuable message. It can often be due to a lack of information from senior leadership or a lack of transparency. The most important thing I want to outline in this section is that unclear communication causes chaos, extra work, stress, missed goals and disengagement.

At each level in an organization and within a team having clear communication means being accessible, available, and relatable. It's ok to not have the perfect answer, but don't dance around it or b.s. it. Say it. *I don't know, but I will seek to find out or for now let's stay focused on what we are needed to do.* This includes communicating with stakeholder partners and customers or other third-party partners as well.

Unclear communication can be perceived as not having a pulse on a situation, not owning a strategy or don't have the ability to resolve (in over our heads). Unclear communication can be perceived as we as the leader 'don't care' about the members who will be executing the work. Of course, this may not be true, but here we are dealing with perception and perception is reality.

When we find ourselves communicating in an unclear way many times it's because we are not aware of how the other person (group) prefers to be communicated to and how they receive and process information. If we offer a message without connecting to the audience or receiver with our direction or intention, we tend to lose them. Being aware when others are not receiving information the way we shared it, or the message is getting lost is the first step to making improvements.

Unclear communication or ambiguous communication can create a two-level approach that we need to correct. When we can break through perceptions surrounding what we've communicated it's a matter of getting clear and specific, consistent and course correct where things may have gotten off track. It will also mean communicating that the correction is in process to ensure your credibility meter goes back up with stakeholder partners and team members.

The impact of unclear communication in business and within teams can cause chaos. That is the simplest explanation. Taking it deeper, disengagement and even unnecessary work can stem from unclear communication. Avoiding conflicts or difficult conversations by using ambiguous messaging can create an even worse situation. Performance management fails when we do not align messaging with the person receiving it. Keep in mind communication is not just written or verbal words, it's tone/speed of what's being spoken, body language and facial expressions or non-verbal cues as well.

I remember a time when my team was presenting to an external stakeholder partner an amazing idea to build a scalable enablement platform for our customers. I was surprised when we got to a discussion point and the external partner started asking questions and was concerned that they were not included in the planning or discussion about this approach. Come to find out the person leading the idea was trying to create a perfect solution before presenting it to this partner. This was the meeting they were presenting the concept in.

When we make assumptions that others will just get on board with our ideas or plans, we exclude them from the co-creation process. When we peel back the onion in this scenario there were two situations going on. Expectations of the partner were not clear for the idea leader to include them and co-create together. And the idea leader was assuming they needed to create this internally first and then share. Assumptions can have a big impact on communication effectiveness.

Make the Shift

How to break through assumptions:
- Listen instead of defending.
- Ask questions. Get curious. Seek truth. Get clarity.
- Identify stories we are telling ourselves. Label them as 'story in progress' which helps the brain to keep it evolving and not fact.
- Extend trust by assuming your colleagues are doing their best.
- Stop and think about all the stakeholders involved. Don't assume a group does not need to be included in a change.
- Double click on pain point assumptions. Go deeper instead of using anecdotes when portraying pain points within an organization or for a customer. This will instead build a stronger message or story.

4

COMMAND AND CONTROL IS OUTDATED

People are very open-minded about new things...as long as they're exactly like the old ones!
——Charles Kettering

Micromanagement
Nicko shares his view on the negative impact of micromanagement. He shares, "From a leadership perspective, there's a fine balance between accountability and overall analysis. So, with the command and control, what we typically see is micromanagement. When there's a lack of trust in the organization, or just from that individual, it just permeates down through their organizational structure, and then it starts to look and feel like, a lot of measurement. I've seen this micromanagement approach really kind of stifled a leader's own view of being able to see where the industry is going three years from now. And I would be a part of conversations where I would question the senior leadership vision because they were out of touch with what customers want.

The problem is with the sounding board we use to gather data in the industry. Are they future customers who want to expand and grow or lifestyle businesses that were probably going to sell in a year or two? The challenge is we can hang onto an outdated philosophy and not evolve with the times. The micromanagement can cause an evasion of our ability to be a visionary. If we don't trust our team to do what they need to do so we can spend enough time focusing on the next thing we fall behind.

Holding on to micromanagement takes away the time needed to stay up on the craft of our industry and the solutions our customers need to be aware of. Being surface level with technical aspects will not be accepted in the future as customers want more holistic conversations. Releasing micromanagement offers space to invest in building the skills needed to evolve with authentic leadership. "

Micromanagement is typically a result of not establishing the right structures and expectations within a team or organization. Empowering and enabling team members (depending on what role they have) to manage their measurement of success is the structure. That means they have the tools, knowledge and know how to manage their area of deliverables and are expected to communicate actions they are taking to achieve those results (the expectations).

Rach shares, "I've had managers who set tight deadlines that are strategic and then I've had managers that are always asking where are we at with that even after we agreed on a deadline. This comes across as micromanagement. It also feels like a trust issue. I almost feel like the manager is fearful of looking bad and engages me from a place of insecurity."

I work with many folks who have lived in a micromanaged environment at some point. If you are in this as a manager of business or people, you can attest to the amount of wasted time you spend managing up yet you tend to find yourself micromanaging your own team as well. Much of this stems from a lack of structure and a lack of trust, but the impact it can have on confidence, ownership and effort is

4 COMMAND AND CONTROL IS OUTDATED

so not worth the nominal amount of time it takes to set up the structures and expectations instead. People just want to be trusted to do the job they were hired to do. They want to be acknowledged for their contributions and given freedom to grow and develop.

Nicko shares "in a culture where everything's coming from the top and you're essentially just the recipient it's like command and control. I find that you are probably apprehensive to make those decisions or kind of step out of the norm. Whereas in a more empowering culture, everybody's been challenging me, approach, and direction. We have this problem statement. Can we do it this way? I know you told us this. But Nicko, I think that's wrong. I love that."

Let's look at how perceived micromanagement is needed structure and cadence. Another view Nicko shares is how a Sr. leader may have cadences in place to review business with executives leading each business unit monthly. It may feel like micromanagement, but the value of this cadence is that Sr. Leader has a pulse directly from the different stakeholders of the business. Structure does not mean micromanagement and it's important to differentiate what good structure is with intent to ensure business is aligning during acquisitions, mergers, tough economic times or through big changes. Being in tune with the organization, teams and into the customers is a great way to create clear and accurate messaging, transparency and direction leaving no room for mystery. This style of leadership allows for communication to be on point up and throughout the organization.

Lack of Trust

Trust as defined in Merriam-Webster is a "reliance on the character, ability, strength, or truth of someone or something". [9] When we feel trusted it allows for a deeper connection to a person or objective. I've always found the most energy and passion for something I believe in is when someone supporting me trusts me to make decisions, create, guide, engage and execute. One of my favorite bosses of all time gave me this trust fully. He retired a few years ago but had such an impact not only on me with trust, but on so many others in our organization.

When we show up mis-aligned to our values, character, and strengths we create a misalignment in relationships and a lack of dependability or credibility. When we try to command from a place where our intentions are not aligned or come off as self-serving, we don't set the stage for trust. We know how it feels when we may not be trusted and how it blocks our ability to bring our best authentic leadership to our teams and business. We also can have this impact on others when we don't extend trust to them.

Often in our lives there are situations or experiences in or outside of the workplace that may have caused us to break trust with someone due to their actions or inaction. This carries forward into how we may hold back trust from others in the future. Many folks have the belief that trust is earned, but this can keep you in a chicken and egg scenario (based on expectations of what it means to 'earn' it). When we hold back trust of our team due to our actions like controlling how something is being done it sends the message, they are not capable, or we don't trust they will do a good job.

Allowing openness to understand how you as the leader can not only empower but enable your team members to do their best and support them in doing so is a great win. Breaking through assumptions which can

---

[9] Merriam-Webster. https://www.merriam-webster.com/dictionary/trust

4 COMMAND AND CONTROL IS OUTDATED

sometimes create the feeling of needing to control how or what is being done to meet an objective is undermining. Release control of the how and focus on what you can do to support your team member to achieve the outcome in the way they find works for them.

David recalls how he used direct communication and openness to build trust with team members. "I sat down with one of my best performers who's like, one of the best in the industry. And I told her, I love your work, but I'm not okay with your culture." I found it to be holding back information, I found it to be not showing up with the right attitude. And so, I told her, "You need to look at our work in a different light and how you show up matters more for me, more then what you do."

"When I did that, it changed one individual, the other one said she's leaving. And that's what I was looking for. You either change, or you must leave. And the one that changed, we now have a great personality, who checks herself on how she shows up. Because she knows explicitly that her leader is going to call her out."

"I think that it has a trickledown effect in terms of leadership that not only are you authentic, but you're also communicating authentically, and you're holding people accountable for authenticity. And that transforms people and transforms teams. When you work in a collaborative team, if everybody acted, how they felt we won't have a collaborative workspace. I will take a team that is looking in the same direction has the same values over a team that simply is a high performing team."

"I used that to be very perceptive about what triggers the blocks. Then I asked what creates these negative feelings? And she said, you know, sometimes I don't feel validated. So now I make sure I look for personal validation in one on ones versus just team validation to better meet her expectations. I'll make you feel more included in this. And so that allowed us to say, Okay, I am at fault, you're at fault. We're going to fix this together, and it created better trust and elevated our relationship. We opened the trust and that was a big thing. And that's just something not necessarily to do with me as the leader. It was something she carried forward from a past experience.

"So, coming together and having those conversations, they are the hardest conversations, especially with the top performers, because you don't know how these conversations will go. But I said, you know what, I'm not going to allow this to happen in my company. I'm going to just address this head on. And it worked wonders. It's been seven months, and it's been a complete transformation."

Make the Shift

Let's assess where you are at. Answer the following with an honest yes or no.

1. You tend to put your guard up with team members and peers until they prove to be trusted.
2. You tend to send multiple emails a day asking for updates from your team.
3. You immediately go into fire drill mode with your team when something goes wrong.
4. You attend calls or meetings that could easily be managed by your team members.
5. You tend to dictate how work gets done.

If you answered Yes to even 2 of these questions you have some room for releasing command and control, setting up new structures and extending trust to your team and peers!

5

FALSE CELEBRITY STATUS

A genuine leader is not a searcher for consensus but a molder of consensus.
——Martin Luther King, Jr.

Approval Seeking

Approval seeking can become a learned behavior at a young age. It may be how we learned to feel loved or stayed out of harm's way. We may have had a bad experience in the past where we were embarrassed or rejected from a group. This learned behavior brought into leadership is a hindrance to not only the leader, but their team and company. The reason is that typically we pull it back out when we need to make a decision, present an idea or make changes to our team or their work.

Let's differentiate between the block of approval seeking and positive participation, inclusion or risk taking. Obviously when there is a big risk most leaders will want to run their idea or change past someone else to ensure they are not missing blind spots or upstream and downstream impacts they haven't considered. Including others to ensure this is the best approach and a good practice.

When we seek external validation because we feel the decision is too big or we are afraid of failure or disappointing others it can create additional work, roadblocks and take too much time to get anything done. As a leader your leadership should have trust in you to make decisions, create plans and present new ideas of change that don't need anyone else's approval. We have value to add and are supported in doing so.

As a leader if you override decisions or actions your team makes, question 'how' your team is getting the work done and tear apart every idea/plan they bring forward you will become the sought-after validation. This culture is slow, not agile or empowered. It takes forever to get anything done and lacks an improvement or growth mindset.

Culture of approval and validation can stem from leadership. Especially if there is more of a paternal leadership energy within the organization. What I mean by this is the 'father' of the group like a family structure is the one nobody wants to disappoint. That leader may not have established themselves as the 'father' figure, but the energy creates this need for most in the group to seek out their approval.

One of the biggest breakthroughs of needing validation was with team members I asked to create business plans. We went all in with 17 topics that would be formed into rough business plans. There was a time frame to complete them, and they didn't need to be perfect. They were however asking for investment shark tank style and would need to be ready to do the deeper dive details once approved. This helped break through the whole it has to be 80% perfect before I can share it issue, we had seen previously.

Another approach to breaking through the need for validation is when someone brings an idea for process improvement to you, and it sounds pretty good. Ask if they have run it past their peers yet. If not, guide them to share it with their peers and get them on board figure out how to put it in place. This can help create a continuous improvement machine from within and override the approval and validation culture.

Authentic leadership has permission to be messy. It's not perfect, it's authentic. It allows for mistakes and chooses to learn from them. An authentic leader possesses the internal validation they need to make decisions, take actions, and share ideas in a way that is not from a place of perfection or needs validation from others.

Bottoms Up
"We need to move from a top-down approach and get past celebrity status so we can create an empowering culture to challenge status quo." states Nicko.

I love having conversations with confident, assertive, empowered individuals and leaders who show up in a way that is curious. They don't have all the answers (although they don't avoid the questions either). They seek to learn and expand their own thinking and allow for more ideas to be considered. There is no approval needed to share. One of the biggest inspirations is when authentic leadership comes through without dropping names in meetings (just to show power, status, or knowledge) or throwing down a card from their back pocket agenda.

They simply show up and engage with an aligned intention or outcome to seek out. There isn't a flash of power over others or threat of controlling the conversation. Teams need heroes within their organization and when it shows up in terms of an authentic leader that is the best kind. Many times, we can become trapped in the celebrity status approach and only view those 'celebrities' within the organization as the heroes.

I also view celebrity status impacting the bottom up in a team or culture. When people feel like they can't question someone because of how well liked or popular they are or are a hero to some they may be intimidated to share ideas that go against either the celebrity leader or their supporters. How many times have you heard someone say, 'I think we should do ____' and when you encourage them to speak up in the next meeting they sit back and don't share? There are a couple of reasons for this including their own insecurities, not having the idea 'fully formed' or perfect to share or based on who is in the meeting.

The false sense of celebrity status can limit an organization from transforming and expanding especially if it's used as power over others.

I remember sitting in a meeting once with an internal leader running a totally separate business unit. I included my vendor partner in this meeting to discuss a potential opportunity to partner with this group. There was a bad move the leader made. That was name dropping someone within the vendor like it was his power over everyone. Immediately, I pulled back in the conversation and so did my vendor partner. This kind of $hit doesn't work on me, but what it did for many other members in the meeting is intimidate them. I sat forward and said, ok I'd appreciate if we can keep name dropping out of the conversation since that won't make a difference in whether we do something here or not. In respect to everyone's time can we just get to the discussion of what it is you are looking for partnership on?

I'm not sure that anyone had ever stated that when he used this card it shut things down and turned people off from wanting to partner. The interesting thing about this is after the meeting the leader reached out to me and said Hey thank you for calling me out. I realized how much this shut down the group and without you calling it out it would not have been the same engagement or outcome that we ended up having.

When we check ourselves on how we are wielding 'power' over others whether with false celebrity status or in other potentially intimidating or damaging ways we can further step into becoming a more authentic leader.

Make the Shift

Step into your worth and let go of needing validation from other people.

5 FALSE CELEBRITY STATUS

1. Become aware of what behaviors make you feel good about yourself, regardless of how other people react.
2. Reflect on and pay attention to choices you've made, things you like about yourself or times you've stayed true to yourself.
3. Before asking for someone else to 'review' your work or idea to feel like you can move forward, ask yourself if you truly believe in the value you brought to it and if you really need someone else's approval.
4. Do a check in when you take on a new commitment as to whether it's right for you or you want to gain approval or avoid disapproval.
5. Take your time before saying yes to a new task, project, or commitment.
6. Look at where you are spending your time (calendar). Have a real talk with yourself. What's necessary and important, and what's being driven by people-pleasing? Decide what to drop.

6

NOT FEELING VALUED

There are no unresourceful people, only unresourceful states.
——Tony Robbins

Disempowerment

"People want to know their work matters, they're valued. What they're doing that contributes to the bigger company" shares Rach.

The fastest way you can feel disempowered is to not feel valued. All motivation exits the body and resentment can form. Today, more than ever, colleagues want to feel valued and acknowledged. They are hungry for it.

It's interesting how many times we see companies trying to expand and transform while expecting colleagues to step up and learn more/do more. Yet there isn't the system in place to give feedback and acknowledge when colleagues are doing a great job or stepping out of their comfort zone to take on something new. I think part of this is the fast-paced world we are in as well as so many remote workers. Out of sight, out of mind.

Leadership is evolving to include the capacities needed to stay connected to teams in a way that is deeper, wider, and higher than ever before. This allows for richer empowerment and enablement that provides the support system to meet the new expectations of companies. It's conscientiousness to have the conversations that matter most to colleagues. It's awareness that assumptions are so old school and damaging to teams. It's mindfulness to slow down and recognize the impact we have as a leader on those working their butts off.

With all the pressures of being a leader it's important to step into new skills and capacities that allow for conciseness and resonance with their teams. The old way of plowing through everything and just get to the end (of month, day, quarter) does not provide a place to celebrate the value each person on the team provides.

> *"Many new managers tend to go to their comfort zone of the business instead of the people. This makes team members feel like tools versus valued team members."*
> ——Rach

One of the most disempowered times in my career was when I had a leader who said, 'you're responsible for the outcome', but would not truly support me from both an endorsement of the program or investment. Immediate disempowerment took over.

If you are in a place of either feeling disempowered or too much in the weeds to look up and acknowledge your team members take a pause. Re-prioritize what's most important and what you need to do to be an authentic leader in this case. Get a pulse of how your team is feeling and what you can do to better support them. Avoidance will create disconnection and disengagement of the team.

I've also seen very healthy empowered, enabled, and valued teams who worked like magic together. They worked as a unit because they weren't threatened by each other. They aligned on the outcome they needed to focus on, and this didn't move because it was too hard. The leaders of the team were constantly ensuring the team members were aligned to the strategy and that we carried team values throughout the team. Underlying core values of integrity and accountability created trust and dependability.

Shame and Blame

Shame has only become more of a thing to talk about in the past few years yet has such a profound impact on us. Shame can show up in us without real differentiation between work or personal life, past experiences, or actions. Shame is typically used as a tool to keep children in line with expectations, rules, and behaviors. However, it carries forward into adulthood and can limit us in how we show up authentically.

Shame is one of the three blocks Dr. Claire Zammit of Feminine Power educates women on how to clear them. The other two blocks women suffer from the most are isolation and lack. These are the most common blocks for women. Shame is not only something felt in women though as I've heard many men talk about shame as well. When we feel we are in a place of shame in leadership this is what the impact can look like.

The most compelling argument for avoiding shame-based leadership is the simplest: Shaming doesn't work. Research shows that shame is not an effective tool to bring about positive behavior change. The behaviors it does generate are counter-productive for learning organizations. Many times, shame is used with the intention to bring an issue or failure to the forefront to try to stop the behavior.

According to the Center for Compassionate Leadership, individuals who feel shamed exhibit increased blaming of others, angry emotional displays, and lashing out. This behavior can have a toxic impact on team morale, cohesion, and effectiveness, and will also inhibit the process of learning and bouncing back. [10]

---

[10] Team Contribution. "Put an End to Blaming and Shaming", *Center for Compassionate Leadership*, April 15, 2021. https://www.centerforcompassionateleadership.org/blog/blaming-and-shaming

We've all learned so much from the work of Brené Brown and her many books, HBO series and videos on shame. She states, "shame is the intensely painful feeling or experience of believing that we are flawed and therefore unworthy of love, belonging, and connection." Her biggest point is that when words are spoken/written to another focused on self like "I am bad" this creates a feeling of shame.

When we don't hold ourselves or our teams accountable, we become an enabler for blame to foster. It starts with the leader modeling accountability, not blaming others, and working towards solutions or answers instead of avoiding them. Blaming can wreak havoc on relationships, trust, and individual dignity.

"It breaks down the workplace's social structures, pitting colleagues against each other and removing trust. Rather than encouraging collaboration, creativity, and support, blaming and excusing leads colleagues to feel both vulnerable and uninvested in their job."

Blame cultures kill productivity. They spread like a virus and the chain continues up and down the organization until someone works to break it. You might ask how this happens and how do people get away with blaming others, teams or making excuses. If it's allowed, it will continue. If leaders are doing it, they are modeling this to others. In chapter 10 we will get into self-preservation blocks but protecting one's self-image is a reason blame can happen.

Blaming and excusing when you break it down, are just habits, which end up creating a company culture. According to Psychology Today habits are patterns of behaviors, and to break the habits, you must stop the pattern. Habits have triggers; blaming and excusing are often triggered by walking into a higherup's office. [11]

---

[11] Taibbi, Robert, L.C.S.W. "How to Break Bad Habits", *Psychology Today*, December 15, 2017. https://www.psychologytoday.com/us/blog/fixing-families/201712/how-break-bad-habits

Be consistent with expectations and your own modeling because as soon as you slack you lose your power in changing the culture. According to the European Journal of Social Psychology, inconsistent leaders are seen as less fair and can lead to colleagues' feelings of uncertainty in their interpersonal interactions. [12]

Compassionate, nurturing leadership is the antidote to shame and blame. Using acknowledgment through observation over judgment is a first great step. The power of compassionate leadership flows from its ability to avoid the negative impacts of shame while also reaping the positive benefits that come from a trusting, enjoyable work environment.

Make the Shift

Turn around how you make people feel valued and how you yourself feel valued.

- Provide clarity on team objectives and how each role contributes to the bigger picture/company objectives.
- Starts with self-awareness - are you blaming and making excuses?
- Starts with yourself and explain how you personally are going to take ownership, being as specific as possible with your technique and actions.
- Practice compassion in your leadership style. This is a great way to overcome shame and blame (and excusing). Ask someone how they feel about how a recent failure was perceived. Listen. Acknowledge.

---

[12] De Cremer, David. "Why inconsistent leadership is regarded as procedurally unfair: the importance of social self - esteem concerns", *European Journal of Social Psychology*, July 11, 2003. https://www.psychologytoday.com/us/blog/fixing-families/201712/how-break-bad-habits

7

HIERCHICAL MINDSET BREAKDOWN

Find out your talents and gifting and invest your whole time into perfecting them and becoming the best of yourself.
—— Sunday Adelaja

Lack of Accountability

Hierarchy can be good in some cases where there is a need for structure in a way that creates buffer and direction. I've seen hierarchy become a very toxic way of running business. Sometimes this can be set with leaders who don't trust their team or each other. Possibly this has been engrained in a company for a long time and the way the company is structured hasn't changed much.

What happens when we adapt a hierarchical mindset is that we lose all confidence and accountability in making decisions. It's our boss's job to do so. Or our team can't make that decision or find a solution, that's our job to do so as the leader. There are many plays that end up happening and I'd like to share some scenarios I've seen in the past, so you get a real taste of the negative impact this has on an organization and business.

Scenario 1: Vice president receives an escalation from their director who received it from one of their managers about an issue with another department. That vice president went to their peer vice president of the

Authentic Leadership

other department. Their issue has to do with not getting a customer return approved although the other department is following policy. The receiving department was surprised this had escalated so high up and asked why this couldn't be handled between the original concerned person and their peer. (this is a great way to break the chain). The answer was still no, and the relationship was hurt, and a lot of time wasted.

Scenario 2: Sammy doesn't like that her peer on a different functional team reached out to her customer and so she escalated to her manager. Her manager then reaches out to the other functional manager. They talk about the situation and Sammy's manager sees the reason why and it made sense to her. Why didn't Sammy go directly to her peer in the other function to have a conversation? Because she was told in the past that if she had an issue with another department to escalate it to her manager.

Scenario 3: A video call is set and ends up with a large audience (many people were forwarded the invite). The topic, however, is just about getting agreement on sending a proposal to a customer. This is a daily task for the Sales reps, and they should be able to do this just fine. The highest level of role on the call ended up being a senior vice president. Why? Lack of trust.

Often, we come across scenarios where we are hesitant to make a decision or own a solution because we fear if it fails the impact will come back on us. This can create a sense of lack of accountability whether we realize it or not. What is amazing about accountability is that when we fully accept our role and responsibility for decisions, deliverables, and actions we should want to be accountable. When others see we hold ourselves and teams accountable trust builds quickly, and we break through the dependency on hierarchy or other structures to get the job done.

Here's an example when I dealt with accountability issues. I had just taken over a new role and team which I was very excited about. I felt like wow this is going to be great and there is so much opportunity. Then my

7 HIERCHICAL MINDSET BREAKDOWN

first meeting with a stakeholder slapped me upside the head. 'Your team is not accountable'. They don't follow-through, their communication is lacking and there is too much protection going on of these gaps and poor behaviors.

Whoa! I was shocked. Really? This was a surprise, but I took it seriously. There were a few things in my mind that I needed to hold myself accountable for and those were realigning expectations, drive for improvement and ensure we had feedback loops with those stakeholder groups to improve the perception and support of the team.

Digging in with a curious mind (I had to because I was blown away) there were a few glaring issues. None of which had to do with not having good intentions (phew). 1. Broken processes in workflow across functions. 2. Lack of focus on team mailbox SLAs to the other group requests. 3. Attempts to gain mindshare through opportunity (and not addressing the breakdowns). We needed to get our house in order.

It didn't take long. A little restructure and engagement with the team to ensure commitment and accountability. Setting expectations that provided clear SLAs, priorities, and role definitions. Then it was about holding ourselves accountable to the new feedback loop issues no matter what - address them quickly and confirm back. We lowered our shields and entered conversations from a place of curiosity and a desire to partner. Not protect.

Disrespect

Everyone in the workplace deserves respect. You don't need to agree with everyone you work with—you don't even have to like everyone you work with—but you do need to be respectful.

Managers should have respect for their direct reports, colleagues should have respect for coworkers, and so on. It doesn't matter what your position is within a company; people should be respectful towards you, and you should give respect back in return. A business that champions respect will ensure everyone feels valued, turnover remains low, teams are able to collaborate effectively, and everyone trusts one another.

Signs of disrespect in the workplace include:
- Managers micromanaging everything and everyone
- Leaders in charge changing their mind constantly without considering the impacts to their team.
- Lack of transparency where only certain members are kept in the loop
- Each person's time is not valued or considered
- Very few explanations given as to why decisions are made
- Eye rolling and other dismissive body language
- People take credit for other people's work or ideas
- Colleagues are overworked without any consideration of burnout
- Smaller cliques from within the organization (we've all seen this even in Sr. Leadership)
- malicious gossip
- threats or intimidation
- giving people the silent treatment

Disrespect in the workplace can creep in whenever there's a lack of transparency. Lack of transparency means that the team needs to fill in the blanks, which leads to stress, uncertainty, competition, and rumors. Be clear about what's going on in the business and keep everyone on the team informed.

Mutual respect in the workplace establishes a positive environment that encourages collaboration, creativity, trust, and loyalty. Respectful work environments are built on fairness and inclusivity. Everyone is a valuable member of the team, and they should be made to feel that way.

Make the Shift #1

Break through the hierarchical mindset.

1. Think of a current situation where a decision or problem can be solved by someone you know on your peer's team. How quickly would going directly to that person solve the problem? What will their leader (your peer) think about you engaging their team member directly? Does it matter? Could you use this as an opportunity to reset expectations to streamline and remove gatekeepers? Have the conversations, model the behavior you wish to see and speak about the successes your team have made working directly with their own peers in other groups.
2. Have an open conversation with a peer or team member about how they will handle a situation or make a decision. Empower AND enable them with increased confidence, practice conversations and walking through how their decisions could play out. Support them. Don't do it for them.
3. Practice co-creation and work with other leaders to establish how each define accountability and how it can be instilled by each of you and in the culture.
4. Make the decision. You are very capable of making the decision and informing your boss that you did instead of needing them to make the decision or validate you. Try it with something on your plate today.

Make the Shift #2

Try this in preparation for a conversation:
- set intention/outcome for why the conversation is happening
- decide if what you have to say will hurt or benefit the other person (how can this prep allow you to shift the way you might say it)
- ask yourself a few 'I wonder' questions before the conversation or meeting to prime your curiosity

During the conversation:
- communicate with transparency, come across with no hidden agendas
- speak in we, us, ours instead of I, me, mine language
- practice deep listening
- go into curiosity mode
- what is he/she thinking and feeling about the situation?
- use 'I wonder......' vs. knowing the answer
- allow space and silence for others to jump in
- focus on intentionally seeing the best in the other person. Keep it human.

8
FEAR OF FAILURE IMPACTS

Everything is cause and effect. If you don't move, nothing will move with you, and nothing will move toward you.
—— Michael J. Fox

Perfectionism

It's good to have high standards for yourself and for others up to a point, but perfectionism is, ultimately, a losing strategy. Therefore, I've found this to be a block in authentic leadership evolution. The truth is that you can still have huge drive, determination, and ambition without tyrannizing yourself (and possibly others) with the 'absolutist' demands of perfectionism.

If you have perfectionist expectations of yourself, you will constantly feel dissatisfied and a failure, even when others think that you did a great job.

If you have perfectionist expectations of others, you will turn into a control freak and constantly feel let down by and disappointed in them.

The 'if it's not absolutely perfect then it's a disaster' approach to decisions, creations and strategies is also known as 'black and white' or 'all or nothing' thinking. All or nothing thinking makes you more emotional because it's how the emotional 'fight or flight' part of your brain works. Especially now, with uncertainty and unpredictability as staples in our life and business if you expect perfection all the time then you will always be disappointed, and your self-esteem will suffer.

Perfectionists use up a lot of energy worrying and fretting about stuff that 'should' have been done. They also tend to see other people as a means to an end, rather than persons in their own right, which can make perfectionists seem rather inhuman. As strong authentic leadership is about connection, empathy and co-creation, perfectionism does not fit well. In fact, there is a wall that can go up for each of these capacities when perfectionism is present.

What's lost when we sit in perfection? There are lost opportunities to co-create solutions, programs and services that align best with customer expectations. There are missed opportunities to build genuine rapport through empathy by not connecting to the person as a human instead of a means to an end. We have the potential to sit in isolation without asking for support or resources we need to do an even better job.

Janee shares how parents can cause us to sit in perfectionism based on their expectations. Recognizing it is holding us back in our leadership and decisions. She has had to overcome instilled expectations of perfectionism in her own life and work. Accepting the potential for failure as an experiment to discover a solution that can be most effective.

She also shares about a leader who was an impactful leader, nurturer, and communicator. This person struggled with making decisions at the speed that others expected or needed. Getting stuck in the analysis paralysis hole out of fear of not making a perfect decision would create missed opportunities. For this leader many decisions became non-decisions out of missing the window to decide. Non-decision can cause us to miss our window.

The perfection block as a leader can impact how our team can flow in their day, delay decisions and launches or business plans from coming to fruition. The fear of failure holds us back from putting 'something out there' to get the ball rolling. Many times, when the leader has perfectionism tendencies it creates a fear in their team who also display these perfectionism tendencies (similar to parents influencing them).

When you relax and worry less, you give your creative problem-solving mind a real chance to find solutions and become more effective. Finding use of experimentation to overcome a fear of failure can help the leader, but the leader can use this approach to break through perfectionism due to a fear of failure within their team as well.

Hesitancy

As part of the perfectionism section, we touched on non-decision or delays in making decisions. There are other impacts that come out of having a fear of failure. This includes hesitancy in taking action, risks and opportunities. In our fast-paced world this has become an even greater impact to losing opportunities or executing in business.

Sometimes hesitancy can be a blessing. Like when you pause at a green light for that split second that allowed you to see the car barreling through their red light preventing an accident. Maybe it's hesitancy to get married or making a financial investment that soon after each seem to fall apart. Often our intuition feeds into these hesitancies to communicate caution to us. This is a good thing!

When hesitancy becomes a crutch is when it's due to a lack of commitment because we are on the hook for something. When we don't want to be held accountable for the outcome or consequences is when we hesitate. In most instances this can become a habitual crutch that can spread across our work competencies.

Consciously we may realize when we are being hesitant and want to take action but sit in uncertainty of the outcome, so we stall. This stage of hesitancy can cause us to lose opportunities, come across as indecisive or make mistakes because we hesitated. The fear of failure that fuels hesitancy becomes one of the biggest regrets I've found with clients.

They wonder if that job opportunity they didn't apply for was the job that would have launched their career further than where they are now. They wonder if that course would have given them the confidence and increased skills to become more credible in their vocation. They wonder if they had jumped on that amazing candidate sooner if their team would have flourished more. They wonder if they had presented their idea when they had the chance if they would have been able to make a difference in their colleagues and customers.

Back to the fear of failure fueling hesitancy, very often it has to do with making decisions. When we don't have a solid decision-making system where we trust ourselves, we tend to sit in hesitancy. When we have the structures around our decision making in place in a way that we can tap into them, follow them through, have a backup plan or just simply use an experimentation mindset to approach decisions we can flow timelier and decisively.

The hesitancy block holds us back from being able to be decisive, credible, reliable and an enabler to remove obstacles for our team. In our world of uncertainty and unpredictability habitual hesitancy is not going to support authentic leadership evolution. How do we reduce hesitancy in our work/life?

Make the Shift #1

Break through perfectionism

1. In what ways does perfectionism show up in your work?
2. What additional pressures do you put on yourself or others to meet your own expectations?
3. When did the story "I'm a failure" first show up in your life? Think way back. Where in your body did you feel this sense of being a failure? Name it (what feeling was it?).

4. What structures and systems can you add that provide for more order, timeliness, better communication of what is happening and to do less work of a higher quality?

Make the Shift #2

Identify how hesitancy shows up in your work/life.
1. Think of a specific area in your work where you hesitate.
2. Does this area include decision making or taking action?
3. What is your biggest fear of failing in this area of your work?
4. When did this fear come true in the past or whom did you see this happen to?
5. If you made a decision and it was wrong what is the worst thing that could happen to you?
6. Pick an area that you could reduce hesitancy in action or decisions and give yourself a deadline to do so.

9

SELF-IMPOSED DECISION FATIGUE

Once you make a decision, the universe conspires to make it happen.
—— Ralph Waldo Emerson

Missing Strategies

Decision fatigue may happen because of overwhelm, lack of delegating decisions (taking them all on) or from a lack of decision-making strategy which we are going to dive into here. Do you get home from work and the first question that someone asks is 'what do you want to dinner'? Your answer is probably I don't care whatever you want. It's because we have been in decision making mode all day at work and we just can't make another decision.

The psychological effects of decision fatigue can vary, potentially leading to difficulty making the right decisions, impulse buying, or other avoidance behaviors. Studies show that as the brain becomes fatigued after making so many decisions, we worsen in our ability to make decisions. [13]

---

[13] Johnson, John. "What is Decision Fatigue", *Medical News Today*, July 6, 2020. https://www.medicalnewstoday.com/articles/decision-fatigue

The weight of decisions, stress levels of the person and quantity of decisions being made in a day can lead to decision fatigue. Often as our day goes on, we start limiting the choices we have in each decision just to make it quickly and with less inputs. This means we are making decisions without the full viewpoint of choices.

Reducing stress and making it easier to make decisions by instilling better decision-making strategies can make a big impact on reducing decision fatigue. This enables a different belief system around how much influence and control over the decision a person has. We will go further into delegation in the following section, but this is also a big part of reducing decision fatigue.

Making great decisions doesn't have to be a burden or draining. Below are 12 common decision-making styles or methods to help the decision-making process. Running a major decision through several strategies can be very revealing! And the process of making great decisions may become something that we look forward to!

1. Logical "What are the pros and cons for each option? Which is most advantageous?"
2. Intuitive "What is your gut saying? What feels right to you?"
3. Relational "How will this course of action affect your team and peers? Who will benefit, who will be hurt?"
4. Priorities "How do the key principles and priorities in your work apply to this decision?"
5. Alignment "How well does this decision align with your passions, values and calling?"
6. Decisive "What approach would most quickly lead you to a decision?"
7. Adaptive "What things could be left open to allow for new information or options that don't appear today? What things must be decided now that you cannot put off for later?"

8. Participative "What does your team think as a whole? What would be the outcome if you decided as a team?"
9. Consultative "What do your team members want you to consider? Would they support your decision after providing their input?"
10. Fear Drivers "What fears or inner drives are influencing your response? How could you remove those things from the inputs so you can make a better decision?"
11. Cost "What would it cost in terms of time and resources to do this? What would it cost you if you don't do this? What's the cost if you don't decide or let hesitancy take over?"
12. Risk/Reward "What is the payoff for each option? The risk? Can you live with the worst-case outcome? What steps will minimize risk and maximize the chance of success?"

Lack of Delegation

One of my biggest blocks going into a director role for the first time was delegation. I had always depended on myself and skills and was regularly attached to the outcome which meant I needed to design the path to get there. What I found as I was now expected to be more strategic and less tactical was that I needed to delegate. Easier said than done!

As we continue down this path of uncertainty and unpredictability in the business world it's important to allow for flow, stay in tune with where opportunities pop up and to let go of what is not working. I view delegation as one of the fantastic skills that will offer relief to decision fatigue and offer more eyes on where the business is headed.

Decision fatigue can happen when leaders take on all decisions in their area. Even when many if not most decisions can absolutely be handled by their team members. Much of the decision fatigue I see today is happening due to a lack of delegating those decisions.

The most common difficulty with delegation is possibly accountability. When you delegate a task, you give up the responsibility for its execution. But if you're a manager, you are still ultimately accountable for the success or failure of that task.

Do these "don't delegate" excuses sound familiar?

"It's faster just to do it myself."
"I'm the one accountable for the decision outcome."
"Other people can't do it as well as I do."
"I don't have anyone else available to do it."

When you waste your time on low-value activities, you're making life harder for yourself—you get stressed, you risk burnout, and you're hurting your team and company's potential to scale. There is also a big miss that happens for your team when you hold everything close to the vest. They don't grow and expand as much or as quickly as they could.

Delegation is hard because it requires trusting others. Trust doesn't come naturally to everyone, and it's hard to build trust when you're overloaded already. I call this the dog chasing its tail cycle. It's hard to break the cycle without causing a miss or failure to happen.

Often, we also get held up by the fact that the person who we might want to delegate an important meeting or project to already has a full plate. Don't stop the delegation process at them. Look at what they are doing and what can be delegated to another person on the team to open capacity for them to really invest and gain out of it what you intend.

There are a few lessons I learned along the journey that I share with clients and mentees who are looking to make the shift from a lack of delegation to trusting their team and releasing control.

As I was on my journey I worked closely with my team, was clear on expectations and spent time with them to better understand their current abilities and experience as well as their potential. I slowly started to bring them into bigger conversations and give them space to bring solutions to the table.

A big help was that I had so much on my plate I was in survival mode. I needed them and as I really got to know them, I really trusted them. They were fantastic! They were committed and cared about the customer and worked really freaking hard. Survival mode meant that instead of working 80 hours a week I needed to let go of some things.

This was not easy however due to my own vision of how things 'should' be done. Instead, I had to really work hard on releasing my attachment to the outcome and allow for the team to determine how the solution should play out or the work should get done. Once I saw their even better solution in play it not only gave me confidence but reminded me that I wasn't the smartest person on team.

As process improvement and reporting became part of roles on the team, I started including members in customer sessions, decisions and presentations to share our strategy. This part of delegation stayed with me in future roles to not only empower and enable my team, but to develop skills and capacities that they had the potential to expand with some exposure and experience. I was very aware of abilities and lined up new ideas to be mapped out with those who were ready for that area.

To me it wasn't about delegating a bunch of tasks, but instead important drivers in the business and team as well as the opportunities for our team and individuals to expand and grow. What are some ways you can break through the decision fatigue block by delegating more?

Make the Shift #1
Implementing decision strategies that reduce fatigue.
1. Think about a decision you need to make now and are struggling with it.
2. How will you make the decision?
3. What factors will make the most difference to you?

4. What do you need to know to make a great decision?
5. What would a great decision look like?
6. How do you usually make decisions?
7. What other decision strategies could you use from above? Which methods do you want to try?

Make the Shift #2

Delegate with confidence and trust.

1. Evaluate your team members for not only current abilities and experience, but potential.
2. Identify those on your team who are ready for more responsibility, have capacity or desire advancement.
3. Map out what you are currently doing day to day, strategically and with other organizations.
4. Who on your team can take on some of the areas of responsibility you currently have? Even if they may not be perfect at first. Remember, not just tasks, but that they will gain benefit from as well.
5. Shifting down. Now determine what on their plate can be done by someone else on the team to give them capacity to expand with the areas you have identified for them to take on.

10

SELF PRESERVATION BEHAVIORS

When you switch your have to's to your get to's your life will change.
——Nick Santonastasso

Expert Status

Why do we go into self-preservation mode? Sometimes this has to do with our environment. Take a pulse on if there is toxicity around you. If so, this is probably the main reason you are in self-preservation or self-protection mode. Another is fear of losing your job. You may have experienced this in the past and it sits at the back of your mind. Many times, this projects as a form of Imposter Syndrome.

A big part of self-preservation is that of being the expert. Knowing all the ins and outs of processes and systems (or apply here what your area of focus is in work). This is mostly driven from fear of losing a job, being called out for not knowing the answer (probably happened in the past) or wanting to prove yourself (fueled from issues with self-worth).

Holding expert status somehow relieves these fears and desires and gives us a sense of confidence. However, authentic leadership no longer views this as a badge of honor and requires curiosity and a beginner's mindset to navigate current/future times of uncertainty and unpredictability.

Taking the behaviors that can come with expert status or know it all comes down to hoarding or holding back information, not documenting processes so others don't have access to how things work and not having a succession plan to prepare team members to take over your job someday.

When we sit in this ego state block, we can actually hold ourselves and others back from advancement and innovation individually and as a team. Think of a time you were in a meeting where the intent was to collaborate finding a solution to a bad customer experience happening. There is a subject matter expert (SME) in the meeting, and they tend to drive the direction. They seem to know a lot about the processes that are causing the issue so everyone trusts their solution. However, they only see the process how it exists already instead of what is possible.

What if you were to break through the expert status by asking a few questions from a state of curiosity and beginner's mindset. You know, those questions that are nudging you in the back of your mind. "What if" questions are a great way to break through expert status dialogue.

Now flip this scenario around and you are leading your team meeting and sharing the plan for executing this quarter's goals (mostly known by you) and someone on your team asks, 'What if'? How would you respond?

What happens when you are or have high performers who don't necessarily share information or offer ideas that will help the greater cause and instead hold back information or push others away. The leader needs to act. According to David Ponraj, he has seen "bad apples who are great workers."

He shared, "The number one rule by far is, if you're a great performer, but bad with culture, I will not take it. I've seen too many people in corporate America get more allowances to behave a certain way because they're such a great performer, but it's unfair to the other colleagues. You're trying to create a place for people to come together.

And so, when you lead by example, and you create that culture that says, this is my style, these are my cultural values, you'll find that people that don't align with those values leave, and then the rest of them get there."

As leaders are shifting the knowledge hoarding and reducing the need for expert status, they are setting examples, and this can positively impact team and company culture. Releasing fears that create self-preservation behaviors can open the potential for new skills and capacities that navigate non-linear timelines and solutions allowing for new possibilities.

Territory Protection

Think about a time you were in a meeting where the intent was to collaborate on making a quarterly plan to review and assign customers based on segmentation. You are responsible for a segment of customers that makes up a certain amount of revenue and profit and is supported by a certain number of team members. The simplest way to explain territory protecting is by this. You go in hard with a case to keep certain customers in your segment because your team has strong relationships with them. You get push back because they have grown and should move to the next segment, so they receive a different amount of support and enablement. You push back hard because you start fearing losing team members or the revenue that your team built with these customers. WHY you are pushing no longer aligns with the philosophy of customer segmentation but becomes about territory or team protection.

Territory protection can happen in many ways including bad mouthing an area of the business that is receiving investment, but not producing as much return as your area is. Why is your area not receiving that investment? It can happen when you are fearful of losing team members because you now have less revenue responsibility. How will you get that promotion now with less responsibility? It can even happen if you are trying to protect a certain structure or process you believe in is the right way to be set up for success.

Nicko offers a great story of the negative impacts of protecting a specific culture, philosophy, or leadership style when it's time to come together during mergers and acquisitions. He shares, "From the seat I sit in now I see three different worlds, three different cultures like A, B, and C. And I always describe A as a product marketing driven organization. B as a finance driven organization. And C as a sales driven organization. I think the sales tactic wins, but I also see a different leadership philosophy in each one of those groups where one is command and control and the other one is more servant leadership oriented."

This concept can also hurt the longevity of a team or business unit when it becomes pigeonholed into a category like 'box pusher', 'transactional proficiency', 'big bank' or 'middleman'. Often, we hold onto what sounds like it fits our abilities and skills at the time but overtime this reputation can come to hurt our ability to expand and evolve. Even if the organization does the reputation may never catch up to the true value the organization is offering.

The trap that can happen when homing in on one area of expertise, brand, or value in order to create self-preservation is that it is short-lived. Let's say there is a leader who prides themselves on transactional proficiency and scalability over years of building their organization out structurally, philosophically and skills wise. While setting up the structure it became about adding numbers (while reducing cost) instead of building technology skills, the value will continue to erode.

Fast forward 5 years and other specialized groups need to be formed to augment the gaps in technology skills in the broader organization. Then one day customers view transactional proficiency as that company's value. What started off as a strength became a weakness of that leader.

Another example of self-preservation or protectionism is of an organization that creates a culture of isolation, disconnection and/or superiority. This could include that expert status or even creating a sense that everything is complex to portray the value and unique ability the organization delivers within the company. Often, this stems from a leader who always feels they are battling other groups, budgets or investment asks. Or it can shift from a place of feeling the organization's role in the overall company's strategy is more significant than it is.

Creating empires within organizations can form a culture of protectionism. Sometimes this can begin with good intentions believe it or not. It may stem from a specific way to enable and empower an organization's decision or power to influence ability within the organization. What ends up happening is the vision or getting the work done ends up becoming protectionism for not only the team, but for the empire they end up protecting.

If you happen to be a leader moving into an area with cultural protectionism it can take a while to break through this old conditioning. It's important to set expectations without alienating the current team, but at the same time continue to model repeatedly what is accepted in partnering with stakeholders, accountability, and alignment to company strategy. Stick with it even though it will be long and painful. If you can turn the ship and break through the existing protectionism culture, you have done an amazing job as an authentic evolved leader.

Working through why you might feel the need to self-preserve or protect your territory or area of responsibility is something worth diving into. Discovering if there is a fear-based issue or a toxic environment driving your behaviors can make all the difference in how you participate in strategic conversations as well as evolve and adapt your strategy and value over time instead of staying in place.

Make the Shift #1
Release the need to know the answers!
- Build trust with teammates that it's okay if they know the answers.
- Identify fears causing this self-preservation behavior.
- Learn something new, but don't share it with anyone for at least a month.
- Share information that is needed for others to make decisions and changes. Don't hoard it.
- Hold yourself back from being the first to answer a question that comes up in a meeting. (This is hard!)
- Ask questions out of legitimate need to understand not as a way to show what you know.
- Create a succession plan that gives you perspective to develop your successor when you are ready to move on. (Break through false ego here)
- Ask 'What If' questions from a place of genuine curiosity.

Make the Shift #2
Release the need to protect your territory!
- Build trust with peers that the focus is on win wins.
- Identify fears causing this self-preservation behavior.
- Identify toxicity in the environment, what is driving it and address it.
- Be open and listen deeply to proposals for change before forming an opinion.
- Give and take if win wins aren't always available. Be aware of how much you are taking.
- Push yourself to your growth edge when it's time for expansion and change. 'What if?'

11

JUDGMENT OF EXPRESSION

If I stop judging other people, I free myself from being judged, and I can dance!
——Patti Digh

The Mini Me Trap
One of the hang-ups I see leaders struggle with is building their team. Hiring the skills and fit needed to ensure congruency and results tends to be the goal. However, what really happens often is falling into the mini me trap. This is when we hire people because they are like us. In how we think, act, speak and take action. Our interview questions tend to be geared towards discovering how much they fit what we unconsciously believe is 'success'. Once we start building a team of mini me's even if we switch to hiring for fit or the team, guess what? We are hiring to fit more mini me's.

Here's the kicker. When we have a team of mini me's we don't have a team with diverse experience, backgrounds and thinking. We have like-minded similar thinking and acting team members who don't truly add value in different ways. Who will only challenge the things we would already challenge, who wouldn't take actions outside of what we would already take and who would come up with similar ideas to what we would already be able to drum up. There isn't someone who pushes us out of our comfort zone or to extend our thinking to greater possibilities. We can only expect potential up to the limit that we have set for ourselves.

Why do we tend to do this? I call this a block because it's mostly about containment and fear. Keeping others contained so they don't outshine, outthink, or out do what we are capable of as the leader. Huh? Yes, if we take a deep look at why we tend to hire people like us is because of two things. Keeping things simple (easy to contain) and self-preservation (out of fear). More than likely, we are not truly conscious of this behavior. Yet it's an outdated pattern that does not align with evolved authentic leadership and will truly hold back the team, leader, and company.

Think of the impact throughout an organization like this. A higher up leader hires a few mini me's to lead their organizations. This crew designs the strategy. When you look at the strategy it's probably pretty bland and does not really encourage the company to advance or take risks. Those folks hire more mini me's to execute the strategy and while it happens there isn't much debate on how the strategy will be carried out. It doesn't challenge status quo or current processes or systems. Then those folks hire mini me's to do the day-to-day tasks and engagement with customers and other third parties. More than likely based on the behaviors, thinking and experiences of the leaders above them they will stay contained in their creativity and will not feel empowered to veer outside of the boundaries set. This reduces how agile the organization as a whole can act.

Therefore, I call this the mini me trap. However, there is a way to make changes in approach to hiring and internal practices of collaboration to help expand how a team debates, discusses, and challenges areas of opportunity. The key while in transition is to create safe space and encourage (without the ego) debate and challenging status quo.

So, if you were to look at your team today do you have a team of mini me's? That's ok, for now. Let's figure out why and how you can break the pattern of hiring in this manner so you can build a team of diverse contribution pushing boundaries of growth and possibilities.

11 JUDGMENT OF EXPRESSION

You're Not Like Me

So often we tend to have judgments (small or big) of others in our organization, team, or other teams. Just like the hiring practices of the mini me trap we can also become trapped by how others express themselves personally and in turn our treatment of them. This can be based on their looks, how they act, their confidence, how they speak and the words they use. It can also be based on their role, their intelligence, and their credentials. These pieces of our judgment tell us whether someone is credible or not. Our subconscious can be black or white.

The challenge when you have these judgments is that they don't just stay in your thoughts, they do come out. Others can feel them or literally hear them if you make comments out loud or to others. The shift happening with evolved authentic leadership is that as more authentic expression is happening in the workplace and more individualism is desired leaders need to shift out of judgment of how they think others should look, speak, and act.

In speaking with Sara, she has felt this pressure of feeling judged across many of her roles and in situations while trying to express who she is and feeling good about how she shows up. Sara studied to be an Engineer in school in Peru. She was the only woman in most of her classes. This is where much of feeling she needed to double prove herself started. She did not want to fit in with the men, she wanted to be true to herself yet at every turn she was isolated because she was a woman in a traditionally male dominated major.

As Sara went into the workforce for a very large tech company both in Peru and in the US, she found that credibility seemed to be tied to how you look and dress, if you are strong and how you act. As an attractive young woman, she felt she needed to prove her intelligence and skills that much more. People noticed looks first and didn't accept her credibility and ability to do the job and do it well.

The red lipstick stigma. Sara loves wearing red or burgundy lipstick. This is like a signature personal brand mark for her. Yet one day her manager asked her if she had a date that night. The challenge with having a judgment of how others express themselves is more about you than about them. Typically, we will judge if we would not be caught dead wearing red lipstick or blue hair. We might be embarrassed if a team member shows up a certain way with others outside of the team, organization, or company (regardless of their skills, abilities, and impact).

I've seen teams built with attractive people both men and women and when thinking about why that overall leader was not sponsoring some very well-deserved promotions within the company the aha came to me about looks. Literally! Because someone didn't fit the mold of their expectation of looks and expression, they would not promote a very deserving person.

I've also seen leaders who shamed those who spoke up about something they believed in or had an idea about. They were told to keep it to themselves or to not express themselves so openly or much. This is why so many women in particular have such an issue with expressing their ideas and voice in the business environment. Either they are too emotional, too passionate, or too assertive. Yet this judgment is not equally perceived with men. Even when they could literally say the same thing in the same way.

If you have this block in any way it will be important to work through your judgments of others to expand your leadership skills and capacities especially into acceptance, connection, and empathy. Let's do some work on this to help you move past these judgments.

Make the Shift #1

Part 1: Identify any fears around how you show up with building your team.

1. Are you afraid of someone being smarter than you?
2. Are you afraid that someone could replace you?

3. Are you afraid that team members won't like you?
4. Do you like consistency and containment so your team can 'look good and be good'?

Now take each answer above and look for the deeper truth.
- Why did you become a leader to begin with?
- When did these fears or expectations form and who may have influenced them?
- When you step into your power center what do you bring to the table and how does that empower and inspire your team?
- What is missing when you are not there?

Part 2: Determine what skills and capacities you need on your team that are missing today.
1. Do you need more discussion and debate vs. agreement?
2. What gaps in skills do you have that your team could fill?
3. What skills will take the team into the future that are missing or weak today?
4. What type of person could push you and your team out of their comfort zone - challenging status quo?
5. Are there relationships with other teams that someone on your team could enhance?

Make the Shift #2

Identify judgments of expression that you have and work through them.
1. Pick someone on your team (or past team) where you felt they were a little too different than you.
2. What was it about their looks, dress, behavior, and speech that created a judgment for you.

3. Based on that answer why is that so important to you? Did this happen to you in the past?
4. If you were to look at their abilities and skills alone does your opinion of them change?
5. How can you release judgment of them for their personal expression and allow space for them to grow?

PART TWO
EVOLVED AUTHENTIC LEADERSHIP GIFTS

12

EMPATHIC CAPACITY

Remember that our true purpose in life is to take care of one another. Our occupations are therefore tools for taking care of others using our natural talents.

——Ksenia Sein

The Nurturer
There is such an evolving gift needed within the workplace and community and that is the Nurturer. The nurturer is full of care, empathy, and compassion for others. Their team is their first focus, but their impact can spread to others, customers, and community. Think of the Nurturing capacity in each of us regardless of gender or whether you have had children. There is a sense of care and compassion for others that is deep within us. It's there when we need to bring something to life, give it space and support its evolution. It may be a solution, a project or creation, it may be a relationship, or it may be someone who is ready to bloom.

Over the past century the capacity of empathy has not been seen as necessary in the workplace or in business. It was viewed as weakness in leadership because the expectation is that if you are an empathic nurturer, you will not hold others accountable or be 'tough enough' to be effective. This has caused us to fall into a void of feeling detached from each other and from our work. They have been measuring this as disengagement over the past 30 years and it's been at about 70%. When only 30% of colleagues are actively engaged it's no wonder we are still struggling with outdated systems and structures. I view it like the dog chasing its tail. It will stick to the same pattern unless something disrupts or distracts it.

That is how I view the Nurturer. They can be the disruption to the same old way of doing things. Plus, there is a desperate need from humans to feel safe, supported and cared for more now than ever. Back to humans are evolving and our heightened need for more intimate relationships (not surface level), empathy, connection to ourselves, others and nature and the authenticity in leadership is now table stakes. There are ways the Nurturer not only impact their own teams, but others around them as well.

> *'When you have someone nurturing you, you'll bloom.'* ——Rach

The impact of the Nurturer is that they develop others in a way that is natural and expansive. Empathy is one of the Nurturer's superpowers as it's a competency that allows you to read people. Building a team in this way can have a significant impact not only on business, customers, but on other internal teams as well. It's like planting seeds in a flower bed. Every day taking time to water, talk to them and give them sun and support. Soon they will grow and bloom bringing beauty and impact to the world.

> *You are a Nurturer because you genuinely show care and compassion for others in a way that is empowering.*

As a Nurturer, you spend time with others to better understand their likes, dislikes, needs, wants, dreams and opportunities. You are a listener and curious to discover more about the people you lead. You show compassion in ways that is received as medicine and fuels sustainability of teams. One of your greatest views is that the people you lead are human in all areas of life. You hold others accountable through your clarity and approach to understand. You show care in ways that make others feel special and important.

Modeling this gift

One of the best models I've seen of the Nurturer has been in a leader on my TD Cisco team. Dana Reina is an authentic leader who genuinely cares about her team members (each one). Dana takes the time to be available, is relatable and approachable. She celebrates her team members: their birthdays, weddings, births, and promotions. She protects her team like a mama bear, but also ensures they are doing what they are expected. She communicates regularly and does pulse checks to understand stress levels and is a great listener. She keeps things light yet focused and has an amazing talent to show care and firmness at the same time.

She is culture conscious and builds high performing teams who stretch the limits of what's expected. Let's break it down. Dana engages her team members to better know them on both a professional and personal level. Dana offers advice and supports their endeavors regardless of if the issue or opportunity is within their workspace or outside of work. She treats them as humans and not only makes great hiring decisions but develops her team members in all areas (confidence, skills, relationships, and impact).

Culture conscious she has built and led teams in India and Costa Rica. She invests time and energy to understand the local culture of team members and embraces their practices while also giving them a safe space to show up authentically. One of my favorite results of her nurturing her team was working with her team in India (while an actual outsourced team - not part of our company), created such a culture that they acted and felt like they were part of our company.

Dana also holds her team accountable, but honestly the natural reciprocal nature of the energy within her team is more about them not wanting to let her down. They want to work hard and contribute because she has given them the belief that they can expand outside of what anyone has ever believed in their abilities or capabilities.

Overcome challenges

The challenge part of the Nurturer is lacking accountability of others. Sometimes it can be difficult for Nurturers to care about their team members and hold them accountable. There tends to be this feeling of opposites. In reality one of the greatest nurturing gifts, you can give your team is clear expectations and priorities. Using situations of gaps in performance or challenges getting things done are great ways the Nurturer can open up listening and curiosity to better understand where someone is at and why they are missing on expectations. It may be something they are dealing with at home or with their health and are fearful to bring it up.

Showing empathy and compassion towards others is not weakness and does not mean you have to give up holding them accountable to do their job or show up with and for the team. It means creating space and genuine care for them as a whole human being.

13

ALL FORMS OF INNOVATION

We define grounded confidence as curiosity + the willingness to rumble with vulnerability + practice. While armor is our greatest barrier to being brave, grounded confidence is the heart of daring leadership.
———Brené Brown, Dare to Lead

The Visionary

A visionary leader is a person who has a clear idea of how the future should look. They set out concrete steps to bring a vision to life, and then they lead a team of people in that direction. What is important to call out here is that there is a significant desire of teams and individuals to connect to the vision. In a LinkedIn Poll I put out there 21% of respondents chose communicating the vision along with listening as leadership skills needing to be developed.

Vision allows for all the pieces, silos, departments to come together in a single way. It simplifies the direction of where the organization is going. People feel very strongly about what they are doing needing to contribute to a greater good or having meaning. One of the biggest ways to do this? Communicate the vision. Provide direction. Bring others into the imagination of possibility and where they have a role to play.

The Visionary does just that. They create a place that may not have been witnessed, modeled, or experienced before. There is a sense of freshness in their approach to innovation, improvement or even branding.

They focus on moving a vision from an idea into reality by utilizing their teams to create, implement and execute the vision. When done well they sort of bring others on the journey in a way that is connected and fully aligned.

The impact of the Visionary comes down to innovation and giving others something to work towards. Hope in a way that brings a sense of meaning to the work that it will take to bring the vision to life. They keep their eye on where the puck is going and not where it is today. They construct ideas that allow for expansion and alignment. Innovation doesn't mean technology only, it includes process, experience, structure, solutions, methods of working and anything that leaps us forward into new ways of doing and being. When their ideas are implemented, they bring new life to an organization that offers meaning and alignment where there may have been fragmentation and disengagement before.

You are a Visionary because you use your imagination to envision a future that aligns with what people and business need.

As a Visionary, you are persistent to try new things and find new opportunities. You don't settle for 'good enough' and are resilient and resolute. You don't give up even when things get difficult. You are bold and don't succumb to the pressures of internal or external policies and structures that have been in place for a long time. You are willing to take risks to define a strategy that will indeed impact and evolve business and the world. You are focused on the end state and communicate your vision with clarity. You are magnetic and collaborate with the intent to co-create. You are open-minded and flexible in how to reach the vision and leverage gifts of others to help bring the vision to life. You are innovative and not afraid to ask, 'what if'.

13 ALL FORMS OF INNOVATION

Modeling this gift

I'd like to focus on one of our contributors to this book as the model for being a Visionary. Nicko Roussos was one of the people I modeled the Logician archetype in my first book. His ability to utilize all three intelligences including: practical, logical, and creative is truly inspiring. I have a strong feeling this is one of the components of why Nicko is also a Visionary Leader.

While his creativity and imagination have designed some incredible solutions and strategies over the years his ability to communicate the vision is one of the best I've ever seen. He connects to and meets his audience where they are. He understands the impacts (market, pain points, internal) as well as offers multiple ways for his vision to be interpreted including what it looks like, what it sounds like and feeling into it.

One of his biggest visions was one that pushed the limits of possibility. Not only did he co-create with others internally, but externally to ensure it was the best approach to a new way of doing business. Without being able to share specifics of this vision I'll share his process for co-creation.

While the original vision was a stretch for many to comprehend, he was able to help others make the connection. He invested the time and was consistent in his engagement. Then while in flight of co-creating he was flexible in expanding and changing it to align best with those it would serve. He then ensured he communicated clearly and included others in the 'how' it would come to life. His partnerships with others established an alignment that was failure proof and sparked new life in an organization of stagnant innovation for a while. Lastly, even when things got tough (and of course they did) Nicko was persistent and focused on breaking through systems and structures (mainly internal boohaha) that were way outdated to ensure success.

This inspired so many within the company and even opened more opportunities to expand and grow in other areas. This one single vision allowed for new ways of doing business and how this company could impact the experience of customers in a new way.

Overcome challenges

The challenge part of the Visionary is when they don't bring in partners with other gifts to create, implement and execute the vision. Co-creation is the critical capacity the Visionary needs to have. Kind of like Bat Man and Robin or Peanut Butter and Jelly. It's not the same without both. When a Visionary does not tap into their resources around them, they tend to stay in imagination and not bring the vision to life.

I've also seen great Visionaries who didn't communicate their vision well. They didn't connect with the 'audience' in a way that met them where they were (understanding today's constraints and doubts) and only tried to communicate a solution or end state that seemed very unattainable or unreachable. Storytelling will be a key method for delivering the vision and the Visionary has many resources around them to help build the story and support them in how it's shared with others.

14

INITIATIVE IS THE SPARK

Like the sand of the earth, your gifts are countless, and some are stepping on theirs without knowing.
—— Michael Bassey Johnson

The Igniter
It may seem that taking initiative can imply a rebellious attitude. However, when initiatives are in line with the organization and its goals the result can create incremental improvements, or major changes to the way your organization works. Often, we see great ideas that are needed sit without an owner or someone to take charge. Think of the role of the Knight in both battles and in chess.

The knight is a noble warrior mounted on a horse and wielding a sword. He's the only piece that can jump over other pieces to reach his desired destination, making him the most unique chess piece of them all. In the olden days, knights were considered one of the most trustworthy and appropriate for a mission. Therefore, knights are often referred to as "knights in shining armor". The fact that a knight uniquely attacks by jumping over opponents is also in line with the old saying that says knights "get by on guts, not gadgets." The knight is one of the most difficult pieces to learn how to play, but it is also one of the most valuable pieces in the endgame.

Therefore, I view the Igniter as being the Knight within an organization. When no one else will take the reins to get something going or when there is a valuable need to lead the Igniter steps in. They are willing to break through doubt or hesitancy and face difficulties to get a new process, improvement, solution, or strategy going. Even if it's been tried in the past an Igniter will bring in the people needed to reinvigorate or redirect the idea to gain traction. They understand how to navigate an organization (people, structure, process, red tape) and are not afraid of failure.

Within a team an Igniter plays a role of forward movement. They model initiative and don't sit around while a topic has been hashed out every six months only for it to sit without ownership yet again. The Igniter may move forward with things that are not fully agreed upon due to fears and experiences of others not fully understanding the impact the 'idea' can have on the organization. This could be fear of looking bad if it doesn't work or feathers need to be ruffled or fear of change in general.

The impact of the Igniter is one of forward movement. They take initiative on ideas and solutions that may have sat around for a while or where nobody else wants to take ownership. This could be cross-functionally/departmentally or within a team or organization. Typically, in Matrix organizations the Igniter flourishes as they are seen as a get sh*t done type of person not afraid of boundaries. They can even create more synergy and alignment between teams when they are inclusive and don't force the outcome and timeline.

By recognizing opportunities as they arise in your work environment, and learning to overcome the hurdles, you will be able to take initiative more often, and develop as an effective Igniter. Understanding all aspects of your job, your team, and your organization's purpose, mission and vision can really help. Being curious about how things work, asking good questions, and being open-minded to new ways of working will also help you to spot improvement opportunities.

14 INITIATIVE IS THE SPARK

You are an Igniter because you take initiative to create forward movement with your team and organization.

As an Igniter, you don't wait for permission to get things started. You are persistent in getting alignment with others. You are confident and courageous. You are proactive rather than reactive. You think on your feet and take appropriate action. You inspire others to get on board. You take the first step to get things going even if it's been sitting in limbo for a while. You help teams and organizations to innovate, progress and overcome limitations or competition. You see opportunities and take advantage of those that others may pass by. You anticipate future demands and prepare for them. You work to prevent problems from occurring. You find out for yourself what you need to know. You strive to overcome barriers. You persevere even when things get difficult because you believe in the idea. You act as a role model for team members who, in turn, need to take initiative in their work or team.

Modeling this gift

I've always been very impressed with one of my dear friends and trusted work partners for many years Mike Perez. He was such an inspiration and influence on our practice and business. Mike was not the type to sit back and wait for things to happen. He was in the know, he influenced ideation with the teams, and he assessed the impacts (good and bad). He also led the charge when there was something we needed to go after and gain forward movement on. His ability to assess the challenges we would face and articulate them in a way that created confidence we could make things happen over fear of hitting them head on was a gift.

Mike also created the structures to ensure that movement did not cease unless there was a reason to stop, re-prioritize or pull back. One of his superpowers is his ability to take complexity out of the pursuit. He met others where they were and gained traction through his ability to communicate clearly and set realistic expectations (timeline, investment and outcome).

Mike is an Igniter because he is the one who is not afraid to take on something new even when his plate is full. Especially, if he knows the outcome supports a greater cause for change and forward movement. Mike takes initiative and ownership to spark up something needed and connects the resources needed to bring it to life.

Overcome challenges

The challenge part of the Igniter is simply that you may appear aggressive if you are overly persistent in pursuing yours/others' ideas. This may be out of trying to break through barriers or through resistance. It may also be due to how much you believe in the idea or solution that your own passion creates intensity around the pursuit. One of the biggest learnings I've found in balancing this is to not force it. Detach from timelines and expectations you have having to the pursuit. Allow it to evolve and flow while including others to ensure agreement and excitement in a way that is not forced.

15

CRAVING ACKNOWLEDGMENT

We are not creatures of circumstance; we are creators of circumstance.
——Benjamin Disraeli

The Advocate

Do you ever wonder why we crave recognition? I've done quite a bit of work with clients around this craving. Sometimes is actual recognition, but I believe most of the time and instances it's more around being acknowledged. Acknowledged for hard work, time it took to get something done, late hours worked to get something done, creativity displayed in a solution or program and simply contributing to the team.

The impact of not receiving acknowledgment can be disengagement, lack of ownership and accountability even integrity. There is a sense of unhealthy competition amongst team members as they are all competing for 'the' recognition of the day. When we hear about team members leaving because of the leader more than not it has to do with lack of direction/communication, lack of trust/transparency, disconnection, or lack of acknowledgment.

When we step into the Advocate gift there is a huge gap filled! The Advocate is aware and brings a consistent and genuine method of acknowledging. This helps folks to feel valued and safe. There is a role the

Advocate plays in safety as well. Creating safe space for others to live, learn and grow as well as speak about concerns or issues. The Advocate provides this in a way that instills trust.

On that LinkedIn Poll I conducted 21% of the respondents shared that connection and acknowledgment were leadership skills and capacities that needed work. Stepping into the Advocate archetype offers this intentional and genuine approach to acknowledgment. Simple messages recognizing the importance of what they finished and how that will impact a decision or how much their time spent was on money saved. Often, we may share high level acknowledgment, but it doesn't have as much meat to it as if we tie it to the benefit or outcome/results their impact had on something/someone.

> *"People just want to be recognized"*
> ——Rach

The impact of the Advocate can not only have immediate effect, but ripple down effects. There are specific contributions to the confidence, wellbeing and growth of others that expands past just being a leader. Making folks feel special and valued can also bring in connection and alignment. The safe space provided by the Advocate allows for truth to be uncovered and opportunity for gaps to be filled.

You are an Advocate because you anticipate disruptors, put up the shield and create safe space for others.

As an Advocate, you are in tune with people. You connect to the concerns and dreams of others. You remove barriers to give those concerns and dreams space to develop. You acknowledge others for their impact. You make others feel special and valued. You create connection and alignment through your words and actions. You put up the shield if you need to protect others. You bring a sense of safety to those in your care. You show your own vulnerability which establishes trust.

Modeling this gift

I'd like to provide the example of Tiffany Embry. While there are many folks who have stepped into their Advocate gift and archetype, Tiffany's name literally comes up in client sessions as being a significant advocate. Not only does she care about her teams and others that seek out her guidance and mentoring, but she has a great perspective across areas to anticipate potential issues. This allows her to hit them head on, so they don't impact her team or cover her team with a shield, so they are not disrupted by the consequences of the disruptor.

Tiffany is a great leader and I've witnessed her over the years leverage her experience and wisdom to guide others as well as her business. I've seen her take on challenges in a way that is all about finding a solution and resolution. She rallies the troops and influences the nay sayers. She also has this reputation of being the Advocate for her team and for others. She has created a safe space for open dialog, working through challenges and being inclusive to find the most optimal solutions.

Tiffany has proven how important the gift of Advocate is in the workplace. Her ability to get the most out of people, help them overcome fears and bring their best self has had an impact not only the performance of, but on the loyalty of her teams. As her team feels safe, they have been more likely to extend out to other teams to resolve conflict or problems. Work together to achieve results and even take more risks.

Overcome challenges

The challenge part of the Advocate is when disconnected from those they are advocating on behalf of. When they assume what needs advocating and is truly not the issue. When the Advocate loses awareness of acknowledging their team members and others a big part of their impact and power becomes blocked. Having solid engagement structures, curiosity (versus knowing) and inclusive systems allow the Advocate to continue their impact in an effective way.

16

SEEING THE BEST IN OTHERS

If we don't challenge the way things have always been we'll never discover the greatest breakthroughs of our future
——Sandi Krakowski

The Multiplier

So much of our work structure and method has been about titles, roles and responsibilities. Kind of keeping us in a box of labels and constraints. As a leader there is so much more to how you can impact teams and the business. Working in the box as an 'individual contributor', fear of other's taking credit for our work and not tapping into our resources out of fear of not knowing or being capable of our job have been limitations. This conditioning has also caused us to isolate ourselves from others.

To unlock more capacity and expand into possibilities of what could be we have to break out of the isolation and conditioning. There is this desire to be more, do more, show up in a greater way. This desire is driving a significant need for a 'coach' so to speak that will help them unlock their potential. The Multiplier is the one who encourages them to do so. They offer support and challenge them to get out of their comfort zone.

A Multiplier as defined by Liz Wiseman, with Greg McKeown, author of Multipliers is one who amplifies the ability of the people around them.

This is a close definition to what I'm calling the Multiplier gift and archetype. In addition, I view this gift helps others to step into more meaning as well. There is a need for connection to what we do and what it means. There are many ways to look at this in the workplace including the impact on others, results and value being provided.

The impact of the Multiplier is seen throughout an organization regardless if they officially lead people or not. They are the one who sees the potential in others and activates their highest qualities that bring about results, change and evolution. They are a force helping others break through inner barriers and blocks holding them back from utilizing all of themselves. They help others connect to the meaning and value they can bring into a team, organization, and company. The Multiplier is a significant and usually silent leader within an organization.

> *You are a Multiplier because you bring out the best in others exponentially increasing the impact a team and organization can bring to a company.*

As a Multiplier, you see the talent, skills, and capacities in someone who may not yet see them themselves. You challenge others to step out of their comfort zone into more of themselves. You ignite power in others. You inspire expansion in others. You create a web of intricate growth and expansion. You bring in light where others may see dark. You amplify the ability of the people around you. You spark the light for others to step into. You push others beyond what they think they can do. You inspire others to step up and give more.

Modeling this gift

I'm going to go a different route this time. I can't imagine you haven't seen the Wizard of Oz so I'm going to use this as the model. It's an interesting story as obviously the Lion, Scarecrow and Tin Man all had in the courage, brains, and heart all along yet there are two ways to look at 'who' inspired them to acknowledge their own qualities. Was it the Wizard himself since he was the one who gave the gifts allegorically: the certificate to the Scarecrow, the clock to the Tin Man and the medals to the Lion.

However, throughout the journey to meet the Wizard and have their wishes granted after defeating the wicked witch they were displaying their brains, heart and bravery. The journey helped them unlock what was already inside of them. Sometimes just creating space and experiences to allow for what's ready to show itself is enough.

Overcome challenges

The challenge part of the Multiplier is when you push someone to unlock potential, they aren't ready to unlock. This could mean the Multiplier sees leadership potential in someone and without really asking if they are interested in becoming a manager of people start to push them down the path. Challenging their hesitations without stepping back to recognize this isn't truly the path the person wants to go down yet. Timing is everything for the Multiplier and when the student is ready the teacher will appear really fits nicely here with the Multiplier.

17

ALIGNMENT IS KEY

Be who you are and say what you feel, because those who mind don't matter, and those who matter don't mind.
——Bernard M. Baruch

The Clarifier
In an effort to cut through the chaos and confusion, teams resort to endless emails, chat threads, and status meetings. But these are symptoms of a larger issue: the lack of systematic clarity that would enable people to focus on their actual work instead of getting bogged down in the work about work of continually re-assessing what needs to get done every day.

Moving teams from chaos to clarity is one of the most vital functions of leadership. Unfortunately, leaders tend to overestimate how much clarity their team has. After all, the plan is already clear in their heads, and individual contributors tend not to surface the need for more clarity as it's embarrassing to admit you're not sure what you're supposed to be doing—or why.

When I put out the LinkedIn Poll on which leadership skills were needing to be developed most 45% of respondents chose Motivate - clarity, align, enable. Based on client conversations as well there is a significant desire for clarity from their leaders. There is also a big challenge with alignment. Alignment of personal values with company values. Alignment of priorities and expectations and alignment to meaningful work. This is where the Clarifier can make a difference. Guiding folks back to that alignment makes this a powerful gift currently.

Clarifying is about accountability. By clarifying everyone's expectations and roles, you'll help build greater trust and increased productivity among the team. Ask, verify, and clarify because unanswered questions are a hindrance to growth.

> *"People want clear expectations and goals"*
> ——Rach

The impact of the Clarifier comes in the way of simplification and directness. Through this effort the Clarifier can help teams line up in the same direction towards the same goal without hesitation or confusion. This helps when new strategy is being implemented and not everything has been solidified or results have been seen yet. They can also help ensure there is enough transparency that alignment can happen for individuals and teams into their work and company.

> *You are a Clarifier because you create alignment around what is needed, strategy, and expectations.*

As a Clarifier, you listen for areas of misalignment. You proactively focus on taking ambiguity out of messaging. You set direction and motivate teams through simplicity. You provide direct communication that is welcomed by others. You provide alignment around what is needed. You set clear expectations and clear boundaries. You offer reasons why decisions are made, or direction is defined to help others connect. You sift through assumptions and seek out facts.

17 ALIGNMENT IS KEY

Modeling this gift

One of the great Clarifiers I've seen over the years is Linda Rendleman. She is always guiding discussions to truth, outcome, and simplicity. Her ability to break through circular conversations and get to the meat of the topic is a superpower. She has been appreciated for her direct communication style. She can neutralize highly emotional conversations as well so progress can be made.

One example of this was years ago when we worked closely together and were responsible for our #1 customer at the time. This customer was very important to the company, yet they were very difficult to work with. Their expectations were sometimes unrealistic, and we were always jumping through hoops with them. There were many folks across our global team who were frustrated or even fearful of the leaders we worked with there.

I remember a specific conversation with the customer leaders that came out of nowhere. They were aggressive in one of our QBRs about our SLAs and were almost attacking us. We were struggling to have a productive conversation because emotions were high. Linda stepped in and diffused the situation. She had credibility with the customer and balanced the emotions with practical, non-personal, and direct questions to get to the real issue. Things settled quickly and we were able to get to the root of their frustration. As Linda summarized back what we both agreed to do to make improvements, she was clear, direct, and neutral. She offered timelines to follow-up, and we left the meeting in aligned.

I've seen Linda offer this approach in many of our senior leadership meetings, especially while we were going through change and emotions were running high. She has a great way to sift through the noise and get conversations and focus back on what's most relevant (goals, decision, strategy, or solution).

Overcome challenges

The challenge part of the Clarifier can be perceived force or aggressiveness. Sometimes this can come in how direct communication is received or through frustration when the strategy or message changes. I've also seen when an amazing Clarifier is challenged in an unfair way it triggered aggressiveness. Staying flexible while connecting others to the facts in a simple way reduces feeling the need to force the messaging. Approaching direct communication with compassion and clear expectations that don't shame the other person will offer a more constructive approach.

18

BE THE BRIDGE

If you want to be a leader, be a bridge.
——Welsh Proverb

The Connector
Connection is perhaps the most crucial component in building a productive and efficient workplace. Why? Because connected teams drive collaboration, nurture healthy working relationships, and promote knowledge-sharing. The more connected we are as colleagues, the more efficient our workplace will be.

But you don't have to look closely to see that there are other types of connection in the workplace. For instance, a team member might really connect with a particular concept or project and take it upon themselves to go above and beyond. Another team member might emotionally connect with their organization's values or purpose and find another level of meaning in their role that previously didn't exist for them. Then there are workplace friendships that are meaningful. Sometimes these types of connection go unnoticed within organizations.

People with good connections are happier, less stressed, more engaged at work and even physically healthier. In the workplace, these links help us learn, become engaged in what we're doing and feel loyal to our workplace. Real connection is about relating to someone's perspective and ideas.

When I polled folks on LinkedIn 21% of the respondents chose Empathy - connect and acknowledge as a leadership capacity that needs developing and focus. I mentioned this in chapter 15 Craving Acknowledgment. This is where the Connector gift and archetype becomes the bridge connecting these areas for people in the workplace.

Connectors don't have to lead people. They can be leaders within an organization who can connect folks to the 'why' in their business or to the big picture. The key to the Connector's gift is that instead of treating everyone like they are starting from the same point they can meet others where they are today.

The impact of the Connector is their ability to help people connect to each other and into their work in meaningful ways. Being the bridge can help ensure results are met and the team and individuals connect into their work with ownership and accountability. They can get silos to work together and find solutions that otherwise would not come to fruition.

You are a Connector because you are the bridge to the big picture and others in a genuine way that meets others where they are.

As a Connector, you act as a bridge to the big picture and offer a practical way of viewing change. You can connect to others in a way that makes them feel valued. You sponsor others to ensure they have what they need. You connect people who can co-create value. You show care and presence to others. You are a guide. You meet others where they are and listen carefully to disconnects. You find meaning and help others connect to it. You can articulate the 'why' often.

Modeling this gift

I have witnessed the Connector gift in quite a few leaders in the Tech Industry, but I want to share an example of someone who displayed this gift in the community. In the 9 years I've known Pat Gehant she doesn't cease to amaze me. She is a Visionary as well, but when I've witnessed her gift of Connector in action, she made a big impact for the Exploratory Lab Boot Camp (Exlab) program we co-founded together.

Pat's ability to help both higher education leaders and business leaders connect to the benefits and value of the program was critical. This had a profound impact to gaining support and partnership which benefited the students. Pat has this unique ability to assess her audience, anchor into where they are and start there with building the bridge to the big picture. She did this repeatedly with community partners of the program.

Pat also had an incredible ability to truly connect with the Exlab students. She showed she cared, she listened, she engaged in a genuine and caring way. I remember one student who was really struggling with direction. She spent quite a bit of time with him to help him figure out his path and understand his options. She then offered to connect him with a few others so he could explore and fill in any additional blanks.

Pat's ability to connect out in the community brought in some unique contributors that engaged the students. Everyone from a CIA agent to a Brewery owner to a patent attorney and many others in between. She is a Connector at heart and sees how each person she encounters plays into the bigger picture.

Overcome challenges

The challenge part of the Connector is when the focus becomes too great on the bigger picture and losing sight of where others are at currently. This can happen when we get excited about a cause or strategy. It can also happen when we rush the role of Connector. One of the best ways to ensure to slow down and truly meet people where they are at is to start there. Ask questions and engage in a vulnerable way so trust opens.

19

SUPER SUPPORTING ROLE

There are no constraints on the human mind, no walls around the human spirit, no barriers to our progress except those we ourselves erect.
——Ronald Reagan

The Enabler
The Enabler is the one who makes empowerment happen. One of the biggest drives in leadership today is empowerment. Everyone is empowering everyone. Yet empowerment on its own does not work. When the direction of the company or team becomes interpreted individually, message disconnect can happen. Not feeling connected to the overall direction can create hesitancy. Lack of confidence to make decisions and choices in one's work can cause delays, confusion and a need for approval or validation by a leader or peer.

When teams are empowered, but not trained or given the tools to give them confidence, data, or access to make those decisions and take actions empowerment doesn't work. As a leader if you do not actually believe in your team member you are empowering guess what? They won't either. If you micromanage team members, it nullifies empowerment.

While there is a great deal of hype around empowerment there is a way to make it impactful to the colleagues and company. It is necessary to put time into creating the structures, enablement, and proper expectations of empowerment in place. When done properly empowerment and enablement combined is powerful. That is why I look at enablement as the super supporting role. It's required.

Therefore, I want to focus on the Enabler archetypal gift. This is the missing piece today yet it's within us. We just need to slow down, meet our teams where they are and assess the landscape for where they can go and how to help them get there. I've seen Enablers in community through creating connections between business and higher education. I've seen Enablers inside of companies upskill teams without them even knowing it.

The impact of the Enabler through building confidence and showing a path that is accessible and doable is limitless. I've seen Enablers create entirely new business models that made things easier for customers and teammates. I've seen them develop teams into high performing teams and individuals into strong leaders. Obviously, when this happens the probability of growth and execution is significant. But it's a bit more than just hitting the numbers. When an Enabler is steering the ship new paths are created. New skills unfold and new partnerships form.

> *You are an Enabler because you open up the path for others to bring about change and results.*

As an Enabler, you remove barriers and obstacles so others can move forward. You make connections that allow for new process and agreements to happen. You encourage collaboration to find solutions. You encourage expansion in an enlightened way. You support others in a way that compliments the empowerment you offer them. You inspire others to dig deep within their own capacities and capabilities. You motivate others in aligned direction. You show compassion in your

19 SUPER SUPPORTING ROLE

conversations with others. You bring forth momentum in a way that is unstoppable.

Modeling this gift

Let's look at Janee Francks in this Enabler archetypal gift. Her nickname at one point in her career was 'honey badger'. All good things about this fun nickname including the fact that she gets $hit done and is extremely credible in doing so. In breaking down how her Enabler gifts contribute to the bigger picture is how I'd like to share this modeling. My time witnessing Janee was during consistent growth in our practice. Our goals were always going up and expectations were too. Here is how she showed up.

As a manager Janee connected and met her team members where they were. She had deep conversations about their path, development, and contributions. She modeled collaboration with other departments to ensure barriers were removed and consistency was allowed. Janee communicated clearly and to the point. She connected with her team regularly to ensure priorities were aligned and energy was not wasted. She worked alongside of them during month/quarter/year ends even all night in many cases. She empowered them AND enabled them to be their best and do their best work.

Janee set up processes and agreements with other groups to ensure barriers did not happen during those peak performance times including keeping systems up while we were closing out business over night. She took action immediately when a team member, customer or stakeholder was challenged. She anticipated roadblocks and plowed through them with grace and partnership.

Janee is a champion with her team and as her career shifted into Change Leadership (I believe is her calling) she has been able to model to other leaders how to be a champion of the people side of change and build the skills and capacities that are needed in authentic leadership today.

Overcome challenges

The challenge part of the Enabler is assuming others can fulfill expectations that may be a bit higher than they are ready for. A deep patience is required as an Enabler. Sometimes the momentum itself and progress can push the Enabler into another level that leaves behind others. Reconnecting to where others are at, assess the situation/them and then progressing forward again in an aligned way gets the Enabler back on track. Staying connected to others without pushing them too far past their own capabilities at that time is key.

20

NEEDING AN AMBASSADOR

Everybody is a genius. But if you judge a fish by its ability to climb a tree, it will live its whole life believing it is stupid.

——Albert Einstein

The Champion
The Champion has become an important icon within changing and growing organizations. This archetypal gift wasn't as prevalent over the past decades of work but as focus on people has increased in the workplace more of the Champion gift is emerging. Colleagues need an ambassador, and the Champion is key. Let's dig into why the need for focus on the people inside of a company is important.

Peter Drucker, often considered the father of modern management, is known to have said that 60% of leadership issues stem from faulty communication. People-first managers consistently communicate with their team members. Transparency and openness let colleagues know they are seen, heard, appreciated, and valued. But a leader's decisions and words are just one half of communication. The other half requires a good listener. [14]

---

[14] Irwin-Szostak, Lauren. "The Importance of Being People Focused in a Numbers World," *Forbes*, Aug 28, 2020. https://www.forbes.com/sites/forbesbusinesscouncil/2020/08/28/the-importance-of-being-people-focused-in-a-numbers-world/

At the root of a purpose-driven workplace is a people-focused workforce. When you make the effort to value and prioritize the colleague experience, your organization thrives. In today's purpose-driven workplace, the ultimate motivator for a colleague is passion. People want to find fulfillment in their work beyond pay. For leaders, it's important to get to know colleagues on a personal level to discover what they care about and how to tie that back into the company culture you are building. When organizations care about their people, they build trust. A colleague's trust in their company has an impact on their overall job satisfaction, engagement, and retention.

The environment that best supports the emergence of the Champion archetypal gift is one that is people focused. It's an environment that realizes the numbers will come because the colleagues are engaged, aligned with purpose, and have meaningful contributions. It asks the questions during any change or along a growth path, 'How does this impact my team?' and 'What does my team need to continue the momentum they have created during this time?'.

The impact of the Champion is the shining light within an organization. The Champion cuts through all the fog with guidance and support. They focus on the people which creates engagement and commitment. They help reduce resistance during change and even growth which allows for the speed of achieving results to be even faster. The Champion creates alignment that establishes momentum. The Champion is for the people even when things get hard. They are the credible force when other leaders may crumble under pressure.

You are a Champion because you focus on the people side of change.

As a Champion, you connect with others to support them being their best self. You help them navigate obstacles. You sponsor them behind the scenes. You listen deeply to individual and team dynamics. You read between the lines to get the full picture. You establish structures that provide feedback loops. You help others see their possibilities and potential. You then encourage their expansion. You focus on the people during times of change. You act as their voice when attention is needed to make improvements. You identify resistance and hit it head on with clarity and inclusion. You think of people first during a change including growth. How it will impact 'them'.

Modeling this gift

Here is how David Ponraj models the Champion gift and supporting the people side of change and growth. "I think the biggest thing I can do to relieve stress for my team is just helping them prioritize their day. That does so much in just saying hey, listen, I know you're really stressed out. Pay attention to just this one thing today is huge stress reliever for my team.

We've had to deal with a lot in the last year, that as we grow, colleagues just keep adding stress. And all stress is not bad stress. Stress that grows you, I love that stress. That pushes you that shows you that you're doing meaningful work. That stress is important. But if you can't manage the stress, the important work also doesn't get done. A lot of the times I've seen others struggle with their work not moving forward or somebody's throwing a block at them today or they are blocking themselves.

Being very conscious about constantly getting a feedback loop from whatever medium it could be. It could be in person, audio only or a written email. Reading between the lines as a leader and saying, how can I proactively communicate back to the team and use my gifts to remove some of those blocks.

When you're a leader, ultimately, you're only as good as some of your team. So, you could be very effective in how you organize your day, you're really effective in how you communicate but if that doesn't go two or three levels below, you don't have an effective team. And you're not really creating that exponential effect as a group of people coming together.

Using the feedback loop and awareness I'm listening, I'm thinking about how my team should show up, and then communicating very practically and not waiting for the check ins we have biweekly. Instead, I use check ins and skip levels to talk about long term career growth, aspirations, and values. I use these spot checks to call and say, I noticed something today, I want to just ask you, how are you doing? I saw this, I wanted to just give you some feedback."

Overcome challenges

The challenge part of the Champion is getting stuck in the resistance. This can happen when too much energy and time is spent on resistance instead of moving others forward. Being able to gage what percentage of colleagues are resisting and why is a great way to stay away from this challenge. If it's less than 10% let it go. Focus on the bigger picture which is most colleagues. Set up advocates within teams to help move the remaining resisters or naturally, they will filter out and possibly leave on their own. The Champion should stay focused on the bigger picture while also digging into what is coming back through feedback loops.

21

INCLUSION WINS EVERY TIME

Exclusiveness is a discriminatory trait of the ego. Inclusiveness is a comprehensive attribute of the spirit.
——Ivan Figueroa

The Collaborator
The Collaborator is one of the most important skills today in the world! We will get really clear on what 'authentic collaboration' means and how the Collaborator does this in a different way than how it may have been modeled for the past couple of decades. Much of how we have leveraged collaboration as a capacity has come from a place of force, agendas, limited diverse make-up and hierarchical structures limiting the outcomes and results collaborative teams can contribute.

As people's skill sets get increasingly specialized, collaboration as a practice becomes more important than ever. But what does that mean exactly? What is collaboration? Collaboration is when a group of people come together and contribute their expertise for the benefit of a shared objective, project, or mission. Collaboration is so ingrained in the way people work nowadays that we rarely even notice when we're doing it.

The role of individual contributor is pretty much dead as most roles in organizations cannot be completed end to end by a single person. Co-

collaborator is the new role. Co-creation is the practice. It's important that collaboration teams include diverse backgrounds, experiences, skills and thinking to get the most out of the work they are doing together.

Collaboration is the foundation of all work processes. As the most important work interface, collaboration's main goal is to let colleagues own their responsibilities and perform their work in tandem with their team members. Instead of working in silos and then meeting to evaluate their work, team members collaborate continuously to make sure they're on the right track.

The Collaborator archetypal gift is the idol in the authentic collaboration work interface. They create the safe space to allow for best work. They set the tone for the group, but don't dictate the how and the what will be done. They think about who can provide the best collective for the outcome. They support the group to ensure connection during collaboration as well as ensure individuals working in tandem stay in flow with the team.

> *"The days of getting high praise for being an individual superstar just does not exist anymore. The ability to collaborate in an inclusive way gains greater recognition in today's environment"*
> ——Linda Rendleman

The impact of the Collaborator is enhanced creation of new ideas, solutions, programs, and business models provides alignment and expansion within an organization. Collaboration increases engagement and retention. It helps bring teams together and helps people learn from each other. It can boost morale across an organization and open up new ways to communicate. Although this may sound counterintuitive, collaboration makes us more efficient workers. Authentic collaboration offers true collaboration that is not forced or driven by someone's agenda which offers more engagement and idea generation and action taking in accountable and committed ways. This leads to improved outcomes and results.

You are a Collaborator because you are a weaver of co-creation.

As a Collaborator, you create a safe space for co-creation. You establish the why, yet you allow for openness to get to the how and the what. You encourage teams to form that are of diverse thinking and experiences. You are inclusive and inspire generative feedback. You lead through challenges in a simple way. You support idea growth and accountability of action. You view your role as co-creator. You reach out to others as your valued resources in this process. You don't create in a bubble.

Modeling this gift

I love showcasing leaders who may not be managing people but showing up in leadership roles. For the Collaborator archetypal gift, I choose to highlight Raquel (Rach) Acuna whom I've seen model this gift for well over a decade. When I think about authentic collaboration that is inclusive, committed, and powerful it comes down to bringing a team of diverse thinking and backgrounds together into a safe space and allowing magic to happen. The authentic part comes from the collaboration being absent of hierarchy, personal agendas or tight objectives that squeeze out creativity and potential.

Raquel approaches others in a way of transparent and authentic intention to co-create. She is not about what she can deliver on her own, but how a team can come together to create something bigger. She includes others even if they aren't normally a part of decisions or creation in the areas of focus for her. She realizes the input teams upstream and downstream within an organization can make when creating new programs and messaging and challenging old processes.

While I feel her many roles in tech have been in more of a creator role this has enabled her Collaborator gift to shine. These more proactive roles have offered space and ownership to utilize authentic collaboration as a skill. She provides clear direction to groups without giving them the answer or the how-to. What's the point of collaborating otherwise, right?

Raquel realizes the importance of co-creation and that there isn't an individual contributor any longer. It's a co-creation team concept that drives innovation, teamwork, and outcomes. She is strong yet fluid, she is firm yet adaptable, she is accountable, yet inclusive. All these capacities Raquel utilizes in her Collaborator gift provide a great example to model.

Overcome challenges

The challenge part of the Collaborator in getting others to join in is best described by Linda Rendleman in the following way; "I think in every company these days it's all about collaboration. Recognition comes with being able to work together to build off the work of each other so that the whole is greater than the sum of its parts.

The challenge is that some people don't enjoy or have a hard time being a collaborator. There are still some who are trying to figure out how to get around it by saying the work is happening through collaboration, but it's not. There when questioned, they look for the reasons why it couldn't happen. So, there is still a long way to go to support those that need to build the collaboration muscle.

Collaboration is an increasing measurement of successful performance these days, and many times when work has to be done across organizations, the collaborations allow the delivery of greater impact, and most companies care about the impact, not the activity.

You can say individually that you're doing a lot of things and checking a lot of boxes with the work that needs to get done, but many times, larger impact comes by working across a team or across multiple individuals to deliver something more than one person can accomplish alone."

22

BUILDING FOUNDATIONS

Life is a balance between holding on and letting go.
——Rumi

The Reinforcer
The Reinforcer plays an important role in this transition from a 'fear of failure' culture to one using experimentation as a framework. Why is this important? There are two ends of the spectrum. One is a fear of failure culture is risk adverse. Very. Including what some would consider simple and low risk activities or actions. Then there is a fear of failure culture built from advertising failures in a negative way. This creates a hesitation to bring ideas forward, share plans or take actions for fear of being humiliated (one of the top five human fears).

Instead, we should use both successes and failures as learning tools. What is working and where do we need to adjust. Given the fear of failure culture also exists in leadership roles this can keep a negative view on both. What I mean by both is that when I've seen a review of successes in a fear of failure and risk adverse culture in a very minimized way as an event in the past versus a learning opportunity to continue to evolve a practice.

Often, we work in a bubble without getting input and then take on the success or failure ourselves (or our team). Instead, expanding to include stakeholder feedback, feedback loops with team members and evaluating evidence in a way that is neutral is the opportunity to establish a culture that is in experimentation mode and forward momentum.

This is where the Reinforcer comes into play. They take the ego and fear out of the process. They lead from a place of fine tuning and improvements welcome attitude. The Reinforcer is not afraid to ask for feedback and especially if it's bad view it as a great learning and pulse to make a shift. They bring the word adaptability real credibility. Their ability to keep teams aligned and in motion towards the strategy and vision while holding space for the present to continuously evaluate is an impressive feat.

The impact of the Reinforcer is all about the ability to evaluate progress and success in a way that provides adjustments more real time. If there is a new program or approach to market in place that has gaps based on feedback, the Reinforcer is typically the one with a pulse on it and will drive change quickly. They don't wait for quarterly or annual reviews to assess what is and isn't working. Their establishment of feedback loops and structures for visibility provide the information needed to make adjustments. The Reinforcer's ability to not take things personally provides a very neutral approach to evaluation. They are a critical leader in helping teams to align their value into the overall strategy and vision so there is consistency in how plans are executed, and results are delivered. Ultimately, this provides more growth and profit impact to an organization.

You are a Reinforcer because you are willing to learn from both successes and failures.

As a Reinforcer, you are clear on direction. You help others align into strategy and vision. You display values that model integrity. You create a space for reevaluation of successes and failures without false ego interrupting. You are open to shifting and creating fluidity in your work.

You help others establish that fluidity. You are connected deeply to your teams, stakeholders, and customers. You seek out feedback to ensure solutions and programs are what is needed. You seek out the knowledge needed to make clear decisions. You establish feedback loops to create a more real time evaluation. You are willing to adjust plans. You use experimentation as a framework for innovation.

Modeling this gift

The Reinforcer gift is such an important role to building foundations. It's the one that allows for growth and expansion without ego and creates synergy and alignment. I'd like to showcase how Michelle Curtis' Reinforcer gift has done just that over the years. First, I'll call out that Michelle was one of the people I modeled the Creator gift off of in my first book. So, you might say 'wow how can someone have both the Creator and Reinforcer gifts?'. Therefore, I'm going to use Michelle as the model for this gift here.

Michelle has owned significant undertakings to create innovation over the years. She goes all out to ensure she has knowledge, information, and inputs in her creations. She also evaluates, takes in more input, and makes adjustments along the way. She doesn't allow a 'failure' to slow anything down. She uses an evaluation of both successes and failures as a guide to building and expanding. She adjusts and she wants to learn.

Michelle has deep skills and capacities that pair nicely with the Reinforcer gift. A few of Michelle's key skills and capacities as a leader in tech have been clear communication, deep listening, pulse checking, feedback loops (with team members, stakeholders, and customers) backup plans and experimentation as an underlying framework. She is passionate about her work and inspires others to get on board. As a Reinforcer this allows for adjustment, agility, adaptability, and awareness.

Michelle's ability to connect to the big picture allows for validation of the track her team is taking (as well as other stakeholders). Her ability to ensure alignment to strategy and vision is a superpower. This allows her to create a space that is in the present while keeping her eye on the future.

She keeps a pulse on customers to ensure their needs are driving innovation instead of someone's ego. She has always led her teams in an authentic and connecting way which allows her to reinforce the value they bring to the company and customers. She promotes values alignment and models this with integrity to those around her.

Overcome challenges

The challenge part of the Reinforcer is when big shifts happen outside of their area of responsibility that have not been communicated to them yet impact their fluidity. Often this can be in the way of team changes or in strategy shift. When this happens, it can throw off the Reinforcer gift a bit and cause for a time to reassess. Given the skills and capacities of those displaying the Reinforcer gift this is just a matter of slowing down, stepping out to reevaluate. Within no time the Reinforcer is ready to go with a new direction and works to rally the troops to make the shift.

PART THREE
INTEGRATING YOUR AUTHENTIC LEADERSHIP GIFTS

23

QUALITIES FOR BALANCE

Everything we do involves energy, personal power. The more energy we have, the more we can accomplish
—— Frederick Lenz

I work with clients a lot around their masculine and feminine qualities. Typically, when they feel stuck or drained it's because they are too much in one of the two qualities. Let's define each so you have a quick understanding of how important this aspect is to integrate your authentic leadership gifts and also how this all ties into the evolution of leadership. Keep in mind this has nothing to do with gender.

Masculine natural qualities are projective, active, giving, expansive, and outward. When we utilize these qualities we have confidence, inner strength, responsibility, focus, logical, support, stability, direction, protection, boundaries, courage, discipline, capable, certain, assertive. When the masculine quality is damaged or challenged it can take the shape of perpetrator, abuse of power, dominance, aggression, control, competitive, confrontational, criticism, abuse, avoidance, unsupportive, and unstable.

Feminine natural qualities are receptive, passive, contractive, intuitive, and inward. When we utilize these qualities, we have understanding, nurturing, kindness, creativity, feelings, stillness, flow, radiance, sensitivity, ease, allowing, emotional, surrender, tenderness. When the feminine quality is damaged or challenged it can take the shape of victim, powerless, weakness, manipulation, withholding, neediness, co-dependency, over-sensitivity and over-emotional.

When our masculine and feminine qualities are out of balance, we can find ourselves in more of the challenges I outlined with each gift in Part 2. We can also find ourselves anxious, overwhelmed, drained, and even procrastinating. Therefore, it's so important to be aware of how these qualities work and how to adjust. Awareness is the first step to understanding what is going on.

Quite a few years ago I was in task master mode! We were building an investment house while maintaining our primary home and a vacation home. Our kids were all in high school, playing sports or college. Work for my husband and I was full of travel. Plus, my job changed, and I was in execution mode setting up a new organization. It was mid-summer, and I was feeling the overwhelm and drain. So much so I wasn't sure how much longer I could keep going. I wanted to be there for every aspect of my life but had way too much on my plate. I wasn't sure how to unbury myself, but knew I needed help. I was able to understand that my energy was out of whack, so I looked for an energy healer to work with. I finally found her in St. Pete, Florida and started working with her in October. She was the one who brought to my attention that I was way too much in my masculine. How did she know? As an energy healer she could sense how my energy was spread throughout my body. My masculine (right side of body) had crept over onto my left side (feminine territory). My feminine energy literally was left side of body from my heart upwards flowing out of my head (Crown Chakra).

As I started learning more about our energy system and our masculine and feminine qualities, I realized there were many behaviors that go along with each as I listed above. So, I started to be more conscientious of how I was showing up. Less task and execution oriented and more collaborative and connected. It's taken a while to become intentional of balancing these qualities, but it has made such a difference in my life and wellbeing! Therefore, I bring it into this section and book. This my friends is one of the secrets keys to authentic leadership.

I mentioned in the introduction about how the evolution of leadership is requiring each of us (regardless of gender identity) to unlock more of our feminine qualities especially in business, but in life as well. As you look at the gifts and archetypes in Part Two of this book you can see how most of these archetypes/gifts amplify from feminine qualities.

Including Nurturer to bring forth empathy and establish relationships in an authentic, caring, and deeper way. Visionary bringing forth a long-term vision. Advocate bringing forth acknowledgment. Clarifier creating alignment across groups, strategy, and messaging. Connector as the bridge between people and to the big picture. Champion hitting discomfort head on and servicing people. Collaborator as an authentic inclusive approach to co-creation.

These are the deepest gifts needed in leadership to navigate uncertainty, disconnection, and unpredictability. Finding balance in how we approach strategy, co-creation, planning and execution in a new way that provides empowerment, flexibility, freedom, and fluidity.

24

CREATE SAFE SPACE

The wall that protects you also imprisons you.
—— Tony Robbins

David Ponraj, CEO, Economic Impact Catalyst on creating a safe space

"I've been on a mission to create a safe space for the entire team. And, for example, with the shootings yesterday. So, you know, I have the whole spectrum of teams, I've got people that have worked in the military, I've got people that actively still work in the National Guard, etc. So, I've got one spectrum of colleagues, and I have employees across the United States, I've got people in the Midwest, so I've got like, the entire set of views that America has, we kind of represent them, right. But at the same time, creating space for everybody to be authentic. And being able to address these because the thing is, if you don't address hard conversations as a team, you alienate everybody. And so how do you find a way to say we all are Americans, we're all going to kind of create the space.

And there have been lots of wins and tragedies, but we know that collectively as a team, I've created a space for all of us to have our views and to be able to express how we feel. I think that in smaller teams, maybe at a manager level, making sure that when you collectively come together, you all acknowledge that this is now a safe space for everyone. The leader acts as the facilitator to say, I'm going to create a safe space because people bring their emotional reactions to what happened at home to us.

We basically have this daily huddle, we've had for about four years, we've never missed a huddle any working day of the year for the past four years, we've not missed one in four years. We have this thing in our morning huddle called you share one thing because you've got about 25 people sharing in a huddle every hour. And we have only half an hour to do this. But everybody shares what's on top of mind for them, that is not related to work.

It creates an amazing kind of openness, when you can share something that is not tied to work that's on top of your mind for the day. Yeah, and that forum becomes like this place where we got to know each other, we've got to know about the things we care about what's bothering people, etc. And I think for highly functional teams, you need to create an environment where you are collecting intellectually beyond just work. I know that some people take it to the extreme to say, you know, we're family, etc. And that's okay. But it's how you show up, not the title or the label you put on it. But how you show up.

And the space that a leader creates, is extremely important to unlock that mental block that they have, that if they didn't talk about it that day, that's going to be on their mind. Right, and it might still be on their mind the whole day. But that's the third thing that I've seen has really allowed us to be a highly functional close-knit team that is focused on the objective and knows that what's on top of my mind, is okay. I personally will share, for example, this morning was very hard for me to drop my daughter off at school. There were other moms in the group that were like, yeah, it's hard. Creating that space, no matter what's on top of mine.

People talk about their kids and their animals, their work, their travel, and their vacations in just that 30 seconds to a minute. It is transformational in allowing us to get through our day and knowing that now that my team knows how I feel the rest of the day, they're going start there. So, when they have their one on one or they have their other smaller group meeting, they will talk about it.

I think that's been transformational for us, as a team, and you know, we're continuing to learn about where there are gaps, and how do we better address those. They go to their growth edge, and they know that they can be vulnerable, because everybody else is sharing. If somebody's like, I just don't feel like it today. That's good to know that we create more space for them that day."

Creating a safe space for idea sharing, concerns, and authenticity is critical. You can take this to another level with a growth container or learning container. Allowing folks to experiment, step out on their growth edge to step out of their comfort zone or to expand their learnings are all necessary to truly support folks on their journey.

25

OVERCOME JUDGMENT OF EXPRESSION

Self-expression is the dominant necessity of human nature.
—— Dale Carnegie

We heard Sara's story in Part One about a judgment we may have towards how others express themselves. We may judge how someone dresses, their image, how their hair looks, body art, how they speak, how they sound, their weight, their makeup and even their credibility based on their gender. Then they feel the need to work twice as hard to prove their abilities and impact. So how do we break through our judgment of how others express themselves to integrate our gifts and unlock their potential.

As the block for judging other's expression is released there are multiple of the evolved authentic leadership gifts that unlock. The Nurturer, Advocate and Collaborator (all feminine qualities) become strengths that allow for leaders to create safe space and inclusion. Now more than ever this is needed in the workplace and especially as self-expression and authenticity are evolving more individually. Supporting talent and potential in a way that allows for people to show up themselves and share their ideas and concerns in a way that is unique to them provides more truth and validity.

A perfect example of this that allows for you to be able to model and put this in practice is Brenda. Brenda was a great leader who cared about her business and team very much. She had been in the industry for 12 years and had built credibility as someone who was a hard worker and hit her goals. She had a decent sized team with a mix of a few entry level folks with the rest engineers and consultants. Brenda had a leader early in her career who was very by the book. He didn't want to hear anyone's opinions and didn't care for extensive conversations about anything other than hitting goals.

Brenda thought this was effective enough and since that leader was the one who promoted her into management she played by his book. As Brenda grew in her career though she felt a disconnection from most of her team and peers on a personal level. She was surprised when a peer would speak up in a meeting about something they needed to improve or something personal. She found the comfort of her expressionless world to be the 'right way' to be in the business environment.

As the years went by, she realized her team members were becoming more passionate and vocal about their roles and what they thought they should be doing. They also showed up in more variety of dress and haircuts. There was a shift going on individually and she felt a bit out of her comfort zone. One week she was attending an event and on the first day one of her engineers showed up to the morning general session wearing red lipstick. She immediately pulled her aside and asked why she was wearing red lipstick. The woman mentioned that this is the color she wears outside of the office.

The woman was embarrassed and asked if it was a problem. Brenda realized how she reacted and that this was so petty. Realizing that this was not something she would ever do she thought about how she may have overreacted and put her own judgment on the woman. She also realized that this was not the first judgment of this woman she had had. It reminded her of a time when that old leader made a comment about

25 OVERCOME JUDGMENT OF EXPRESSION

Brenda's makeup although Brenda had very simple makeup on. From that day on she toned it down even more almost to barely wearing anything still to this day.

Brenda started thinking about her team members and some of the judgments she had towards their clothes, hair, hobbies and even cars they drove. Anything that made them unique. As she thought of each of these judgments there were a few that came from the place of being embarrassed or called out in the past for doing something similar. Others she realized were out of envy. She was envious of some of the cars the team members drove. She was envious of the freedom some of them had as they were not married or had children (yet).

As Brenda worked through these scenarios in her head, she realized how petty these things were and most did not actually have anything to do with the people on her team, but that she was trying to mold them to be just like her. She started to become more aware of her judgments back the office. As she began to work through her judgment block, she felt a new desire to connect with her team members. She felt more empathy towards them, started asking about how they were really doing. She started putting effort into genuinely acknowledging them. She even started collaborating with them to get their ideas and input.

The story of Brenda is a common theme. The shift happening with self-expression in the workplace is extremely important as we focus on authentic leadership and authenticity in the workplace. Leaders unblocking their judgments and biases is even more important to really support the growth opportunities and potentials their teammates have especially when they show up in their authentic skin.

26

INVEST IN CONNECTIONS

A business has to be involving, it has to be fun, and it has to exercise your creative instincts.
—— Richard Branson

Stephen Tessitore, Director, Cisco on investing in connections
As you grow in influence and career stature, it's tempting to make social decisions that revolve around your work calendar. Early meetings or late work tend to take priority quickly and seem like the most important things in the world on any given day. Add a partner and a family to the mix and it's easy to find yourself in your 30's with absolutely no real friends anymore.

Sure, you might have people you could call who would be there for you or family you are close with who would offer you an ear or some advice. But without real and dedicated effort, you will surely lack the real fulfillment that comes in a genuine community of like-minded people.

It's not enough and it's not fair to put the pressure for this type of support onto a partner, a close relative, a sibling. Those relationships are tied into so many other emotional structures, riddled with history and baggage and simply not the same thing.

As a full-blown adult, you get to choose who these friends are, you aren't stuck with anyone out of convenience or proximity. Sure, it's nice to be casual friends with the other parents at soccer practice, or with the spouse of your partner's best friend, but those are relationships you might feel forced into out of convenience. They stay on the surface, take little effort, and might only rarely yield true connection.

So, how do you do this?

Here are some rules for building rewarding friendships:

1. Be real. To build relationships that can help you through life you have to share your actual life, not the Instagram version of it. Put yourself out there.
2. Be genuine. Don't incessantly talk about yourself, instead really listen, and really and truly care.
3. Find common interests. If you're a married parent, connect with other married parents. It's a great way to start quality conversations and seek wisdom for shared struggles.
4. Meet weekly. Treat it like a calendar appointment. (You don't miss any of those, do you?)
5. Offer support. If your friend champions an important cause, it should be your important cause too. If they run a business, you should understand and support it where possible.

Here's the kicker, it might not always work. You might find that you don't have much in common after all, or that the person you invested in really doesn't want the same things you do in life. No problem, move on, keep going. You don't have to be forever dedicated and loyal to someone you had coffee with 3 times.

Its effort, but there is no measurement that accurately describes the power of community in your life and no way to express the feeling of being genuinely supported by others.

Great friends motivate us, they push us to be better, they hold us accountable. Go be one and you'll find many.

What is genuinely interesting about Stephen's approach to connection is that community is becoming something we are craving. Deeper, more intimate connections that bring fulfillment and value over surface level and outside of our family. It doesn't stop with friends outside of work though.

As we fulfill connections in our personal life it becomes glaring if we don't also have some deeper connections inside the workplace as well. It doesn't have to be about hitting up happy hour or going on vacations together. It can simply be about a trusting circle of connections with a common interest, a BRG (Business or Employee Resource Group) or a team where trust is a significant part of working in a healthy climate.

Bringing your Connector gift out can simply be a matter of stepping outside of your familiar comfort zone to meet new people who have similar causes (inside/outside of the company) or a common interest or passion inside of the company. As an authentic leader this gift is not about manipulating or having an agenda (based on what you want). It's about seeing opportunities today that are not being connected whether it's people who can come together to better support each other, find a better solution or opportunities not being implemented today.

The role of Connector brings depth to a team, individuals, and a culture. They offer a sense of simplicity and flow and provide a model for stepping outside of their comfort zone to bridge together people or things that will build a bigger and better tomorrow. Our souls are craving this gift to come out!

27

EMPOWERED INNOVATION

Innovation distinguishes between a leader and a follower.
—— Steve Jobs

Jesse Gott, Director IT/Marketing on empowerment and enablement

Jesse started with a well-established small company where most of the processes and way of doing business was in place for 20 years. At first, his perception of the company was that there were too many chiefs, not much group collaboration about decisions (mostly authoritative from the top) yet those making decisions were a bit out of touch and no one challenged status quo. Probably why processes and systems were not innovating much. He decided he didn't want to sit back and just be status quo. He taught himself new skills and started challenging old processes with new ways to achieve the outcome. He also brought proposals for new systems and approaches to market. Slowly he found his ideas being accepted and he was able to put them in place.

Jesse realized his role as Connector would be critical to help bridge the current understanding of how things were done and the future potential with new solutions (systems and processes). He continues today to be the Connector as adoption of new processes and cycles of success metrics have painted a bigger story of where the company can expand into. This role was also about connecting people from different departments wearing multiple hats and a bit isolated from working together to enhance end to end solutions within the company.

Using his Collaborator gifts, Jesse would build a plan with other departments so they would have buy-in and input on the how to. He didn't do this by some hierarchical agenda-based approach, it was inclusive and open on the solution. Jesse utilized his Clarifier gifts to get everyone really clear on what they were doing towards the outcome and ideas on how to measure success. He would read up to the leadership team to ensure support and to remove any barriers and bring the pieces together in a big picture way so others could understand how everything would work together.

Over time, he was able to influence a culture of empowerment and continuous improvement. How did he do it? Jesse views every single new person who starts at the company as a gold mine for assessing if there might be a better way. They come in with fresh eyes. So, Jesse has instilled a process to bring ideas forward early on so opportunities to experiment with their ideas is not missed after they have been there and used to existing processes. This empowerment and enablement (happen when their ideas get implemented) has become the culture.

Jesse's mentality of nothing is set in stone (including his ideas) has given a major shift in culture and ownership across departments. He even created his own position due to his capacity to connect the dots internally creating big picture solutions. As a Connector he continues to bridge to that big picture as well as to be the bridge between departments. As Clarifier he challenges status quo and pushes the innovation internally in a way that is succinct and aligned.

28

NURTURING LEADERSHIP

Management is about arranging and telling. Leadership is about nurturing and enhancing.

—— Tom Peters

Deena Piquion, CMO, Xerox on empathy in leadership

"I think the role of a leader and the attributes of a successful leader today, what is truly needed to engage people in our workforce now is so different than what we were used to in the past. I've seen the leaders that change because they think that every promotion or expanded role makes them a little bit better or more important than other people on their teams. And that comes through in what they do and how they lead.

I think, they'll be remiss at some point because they will lose the engagement and motivation of their teams. It's just not the way to get people motivated to work alongside you. I've seen people who think the rules don't apply to them as a leader. The rule is different for them because they're the boss, and they expect their teams to be okay with it but, I've never met a team member who thought it was okay.

It's not the model I want to provide to my team. And so, for me, it's always been about pausing and ensuring I ask myself how I would feel. Or how did I feel when I saw that? Because I've seen it many times. And I know how bad it made me feel, to watch somebody break the rules that we were all supposed to follow. But they didn't have to follow them because they were the leader or the boss. So, I took how it made me feel, as an employee as a team member and I said, I don't ever want people to feel that way about what I'm doing and how I'm modeling behavior with the team.

They need to feel that we're in this together, that we work together, alongside each other. And sure, yes, I have a different title, and with that title comes the weight of making certain decisions. Sometimes, I must be the referee or the tiebreaker and make decisions based on the data, the arguments and what I believe is the best course for the team and business. But it doesn't mean that I'm any better than anyone else on my team, it just means I'm doing what is expected of me now.

And I think that that's what's so powerful about empathy, empathy as a leader is being able to put yourself in your team's shoes. And so, I always try to use my own personal and professional experiences and how that's made me a more empathetic person, coworker, and leader. I knew early on what I didn't want to model in leadership, and it took me some time find my own style but once I did, my leadership style became as important as my expertise, capabilities, or track record."

People are reevaluating their relationship with work in the wake of the pandemic. Some are deciding life's too short to leave their spirit at the door and endure long workdays just to bring home a paycheck. They want an environment that nourishes them in a profound way.

As leadership evolves more significantly one of the biggest capacities that has become a requirement is more nurturing. You can look at nurturing as incubating, creating, and connecting through empathy. Acknowledging how another person feels is one of the greatest connections we can have with another. Putting yourself in their place like Deena speaks of above is one way of truly connecting authentically.

As we nurture a business we listen to customers and determine what adjustments to make to grow the business. As we are creating new solutions or messaging, we listen to the audience/users for guidance to ensure it's the solution or message that is needed. As we are creating and nurturing innovation, we stay in touch with how this is solving a problem for users and how valuable they find it. As we are nurturing teams, we listen to colleagues to gain a pulse of their needs to meet them where they are at.

Behaviors of an empathetic leader are practiced in asking rather than telling, listening rather than speaking, and serves rather than commands. The leader cares about people's concerns and doesn't interpret concerns as resistance. They are receptive to feedback and don't overreact to people's questions or concerns.

Modeling empathy in a nurturing leadership style is very much an authentic and genuine approach. As we are re-learning how to be empathetic and to use this in our nurturing of our team members there are a few tips that can make help you come from a more authentic and trusting place. [15]

1. **Self-discovery and awareness.** Becoming an empathetic leader starts with having excellent self-awareness. This requires doing inner work on understanding your motivators, your temperament, and your personality style. It also includes knowing your communication style, your reaction to feedback, and how your values shape your behavior.
2. **Understand others.** Intentionally understand your team members. This includes improving your communication skills, such as being curious in conversations instead of being defensive or aggressive. It also includes learning how to eliminate fear in your interactions with your people—trust cannot survive if there is fear in a relationship. Building trust with your people is essential if

---

[15] Conley, Randy, "5 Ways to Lead with Empathy" *Leading with Trust*, https://leadingwithtrust.com/2022/06/12/5-ways-to-lead-with-empathy/

you're to be an empathetic leader. They must know you are on their side, and you mean them no harm. You must show them your role as a leader is to help them succeed.

3. **Be compassionate.** Empathetic leaders are compassionate and extend grace to others. They know how to walk a mile in someone else's shoes while fulfilling expectations of their company. Leaders must balance compassion with clear expectations that are understood by every team member. Leaders who are empathetic place great importance on creating psychological safety—an environment where a person feels free to speak their mind, take risks, and admit mistakes without fear of being punished or reprimanded.

4. **Set boundaries.** Empathetic leaders know how to set clear boundaries that benefit everyone, such as letting people know how many hours a day they're supposed to work or that sending late-night emails is inappropriate. When everyone has clarity on work boundaries—including rules and expectations—there is tremendous safety and freedom. Boundaries create a guardrail, so people don't unduly sacrifice themselves to accomplish something. Boundaries also promote autonomy. They let people know what they can and can't do.

29

CHAMPIONING PEOPLE

Champions are made from something they have deep inside of them - a desire, a dream, a vision.
——Mahatma Gandhi

Championing people is becoming one of the critical capacities in leadership. This includes how we champion the people side of change, navigating and shifting resistance. During a conversation with Janee Francks, she reminded me of a great leader who exemplifies the skills and capacities that almost simplified many complex situations. Heather Murray, Chief Channel Officer has taken on many unique and very challenging responsibilities over the years.

This includes joint venture partnerships and struggling business units. Heather is a fearless leader who has taken on unchartered areas of the business where others did not have experience or simply struggled to turn around and be successful. Although Heather herself may not have had the experience needed to reach the goals the organization was looking to achieve, she consistently leads with confidence and courage. She would go in knowing it would be a challenge but would not let that stop her.

Heather always displayed the Challenger archetype (gift) from my first book, and I always looked up to her for her courage and challenging status quo. We even went to bat together a few times in our careers where I was able to learn close up and view her style. The role of Challenger stirred the pot sometimes. We have compared notes about doing so and how others reacted. In the past, bringing to the table things that needed to be changed was typically hit by criticism or shunning. Yep shunning. That has never stopped either of us from honing our skills and learning how to influence an outcome. Leaders who behold the Challenger gift AND the Champion are the leaders of the future!

As Janee reflects on some of the qualities Heather brought into the team Janee was on, she shared specifics that were very resonant of the Champion archetypal gift. "Heather is confident and smart, quick on her feet. She holds her own with C-level folks and is to the point. She doesn't bull$hit! She has built her credibility by being straight up, accountable and doesn't give up on finding a solution.

She can quickly read a room and assess where resistance and least resistance resides. Heather can determine how to connect with both groups in a way that establishes trust and keeps it real. She doesn't hide from the resistors. She feels they are very important to the mission and need to be understood. Many times, when she just has a conversation with them, the resistance subsides. That's all it takes, a conversation with listening ears and a little empathy."

One of Heather's qualities of being a Champion is that of her transparency. She doesn't just let things flow downhill and cause stress and chaos, but she has always been very open with her teams to ensure they know where they stand and where they fit in (company, strategy).

Her proactive and intentional communication style is all about clarity. She puts effort into ensuring her team is aligned and able to do their job. As she determines barriers to remove, she also assesses what enablement is needed to give her team not only the empowerment to expand their impact but feel enabled to do so as well.

According to Janee's choice of words Heather is a 'people collector'. I love this term as it's deeper than Networker or Influencer. It's about building a collection of skills, capacities and abilities that can influence and solution for tough businesses. Those can only come from people. Most jobs nowadays cannot simply be done end to end by an individual. We all depend on others to help get the job done. In many cases this is more complex than being able to complete the job on our own. Heather's collection of people offers her and her team the support and resources to not only get the job done, but to do it in a more efficient and effective way.

Heather is a Multiplier, but how she does it is exemplary of being a Champion. She gets her hands dirty while guiding teams through the mud in a way that makes it feel like a day at the spa. She builds the support and influences breaking down barriers in a way of a true Champion. She has impacted many businesses and teams and is a model for how to do this in the modern world and business.

Bringing out the Champion in you is simply a matter of figuring out how you can become more connected to the teams and people on them, how to navigate resistance and how to establish extreme clarity and alignment through your words and actions. The Champion is of the people, not just the business or company.

30

FINDING AUTHENTIC LEADERSHIP

The single biggest problem in communication is the illusion that it has taken place.
——George Bernard Shaw

Linda Rendleman, VP Microsoft, shares her journey to authentic leadership

"As I think about what it took for me to become a truly authentic leader, I realize it was MANY lessons over MANY roles throughout my career that helped me become the leader I am today.

When I took on my first manager role, I didn't think about it as leadership, and, honestly, I really disliked the job, because I looked at it as an administrative task to oversee other team members accountabilities. I wasn't connecting the dots in how I needed to show up as a leader at that point. Truth be told, I only became a manger because I was told I needed to have management experience in order to get into field sales, and sadly I was too immature in my career to think about taking the learnings from that role to build on my skills overall.

When I returned to a leadership role it was as an inside sales director, and fortunately I had matured, and cared more about connecting with the team. I still looked to other leaders to define what it took to be a successful leader, as I didn't yet have enough confidence to think I could just lead with my own style and that would be enough. I worked to feel comfortable to just be me in the role and build connections with the team in ways I didn't see happening with other leaders, which helped me build the confidence I needed to grow as a leader. I made team meetings more personal and helped people feel more connected. I started acting with the qualities of a servant leader before I knew what it meant, and it felt good. I wanted to act in a way everyday that allowed the team to be able to bring their best. I enjoyed this leadership role immensely more than the first.

After spending time in another individual contributor role as a global director at a new company, I learned that even when you aren't directly managing people, you are still serving as a connector and an enabler and influencing for greater impact, which was another great lesson.

In my subsequent leadership roles my insecurities got the best of me again. In one role I felt out of my depth and had an incredible amount to learn. I constantly questioned my ability to do the job. I had so much insecurity that I decided my best course of action was to do whatever my leader told me to do and if I just modeled their leadership it would allow me to be successful in the role. The problem is that it was so inauthentic to who I am that I showed up worse than in any leadership position that I'd had previously. It was an incredibly hard lesson, because I knew I wasn't doing a good job, but I couldn't figure out how to shift and change.

In my next role, I was able to regroup, and realized I was capable of better. I started showing up from a true authentic leadership perspective. I knew that I needed to be truer to me, and my confidence started to build and grow. I realized that making people feel seen, heard, and acknowledged had an incredible impact. Remembering small details about conversations that really resonated with people had built stronger performance because people felt valued. I was able to build and scale teams by setting a tone from the top about the importance of prioritizing the needs of the team and building leadership capability based on those same principles.

My focus now is to create a culture for a team where everyone feels valued and able to contribute their best. I work to be authentic to who I am while also welcoming other styles that contribute to that same goal, albeit not in the same way. It feels great, and being a leader is now my favorite part of the work I do. The connection that I form with people in my team and across the organization gives me so much energy. Having the confidence to be myself, being in a service mindset, championing inclusivity, and encouraging others to do the same, creates a high-performing team where people are excited to learn, grow, and contribute."

31

MY LEADERSHIP JOURNEY

Compliance does not foster innovation, trust does.
——Stephen R. Covey

Michelle Curtis, Director, Microsoft, on trust and vulnerability in leadership

"I've had the privilege of working in a leadership role since 2014 and my style, presence, approach to this role has evolved over these last 8 years due to experiences and learnings from those around me, including my teams, friendships, family, peers, leaders, mentors, and sponsors. The most successful teams I've led have one commonality. Trust.

This trust isn't just built when you step into a role but comes from you as a leader showing your own vulnerability, that you are here as your team's biggest supporter, one that will not only lead them into a proverbial battle, but you are there fighting by their side. Early in my career, and I still see this today with some leadership, that vulnerability is looked at as a weakness, but I've learned in my own personal experiences that to be the complete opposite.

Empathy, vulnerability, and transparency break down the barriers to truly help create an atmosphere of trust, which in turn enables a safe space

Authentic Leadership

for the team, and individuals to be creative and thrive, knowing that you as a leader are in it with them.

You may work in a corporate environment and have the biggest target in the world to hit, but if you don't change your thinking around how you lead your team, you will never ignite transformation and hit the growth you need to. Trust = Speed

In my personal journey, I've experienced team members go through joyous moments, creating life, starting marriage or partnership, grievance of loss of loved ones, sadness, divorce, and I with great sadness experienced one of my own direct reports take her own life. This is the experience that personally changed my life, as a leader, and as a person. As a leader and friend, you need to be there to get through this and grieve yourself, yet also support your team (which I see as a family) through their own individual grieving process as well. I showed personal trust in my team, allowing them to see my own grief, guilt, sadness, and need for support as well.

This experience created a bond, although through loss, which brought the team together in a way that I've never experienced before. This was in empathy, vulnerability, trust, and support. And how leadership shows up in these moments, defines great leadership from unfortunate leadership.

How you show up for not just the business, or the team as a collective, but how you show up for each individual person you lead is the most important thing you can ever do in your role and in life. This is how you ignite positivity and growth in those around you. Then you get to experience, in my opinion, the greatest joys of leadership; watching those you lead create, take risks, and support each other, and attain their own personal and professional success.

When your team trusts you as a leader and each other, they believe in your vision, and will stand behind you through the ups, the downs, the wins, and the losses. And even when they no longer directly work for you, they will continue life-long relationships, reach out to you for sponsorship, for support, guidance, and to talk through situations. To me personally, being in a position of leadership is a gift, and one that I cherish every day."

32

YOUR AUTHENTIC LEADERSHIP

Anyone who follows their internal compass can become an authentic leader.
——Bill George

The future structure in organizations will not be dependent on some genius person who designs the perfect one. Successful organizations will be based on evolved authentic leadership skills and capacities of the members of the organization. Notice I didn't say 'leaders' from a title perspective. Titles could mostly disappear other than identifying the skills, area of responsibility or actions that person owns in the organization.

Instead, leadership spreads across an organization. Hierarchical structures will flatten (not all the way but will skinny down). Most matrix organizations will finally figure out how to reduce the confusion and overlap or gaps once their leaders fully embrace authentic leadership gifts and take on more effective capacities of the Collaborator, Connector, Enabler and Multiplier.

This is especially the case for flatter organizations with more self-management teams. Many startups have taken on this structure for instance, but without the evolved leadership capacities and skills will be difficult for those self-managed teams to be effective across the organization, have clear and aligned direction and to truly own a component of the company's process and results. [16]

As companies provide the space, enablement, and alignment of evolved authentic leadership skills and capacities within there will be a shift in how work is done, how people are valued, and products and services are offered. Labels like individual contributor will only be held by true individual contributors who can execute their job end to end by themselves. For all others the role of co-creator and co-collaborator will be accepted and played. Dispersed and decentralized teams will be a norm and connection will happen more virtually than in person.

As a leader, reflection and self-awareness are more important than ever, but even more so is awareness around you. Of your team, leaders, customers, and culture. What are the needs and wants whispering around you? How can you help in a way that creates engagement, trust, and action? It's time for you to show up in your full authentic leadership.

When you can work through the blocks, old behaviors and patterns of outdated leadership styles and start unlocking your authentic leadership gifts you will find huge shifts in you personally. You will magnetize connection and find ease in leading your team and business. The key to integrating your authentic leadership gifts into a changing environment is to release your resistance and fear. Anytime we feel something new coming up in a courageous and confident way we may have our little protector (our subconscious or ego) come in and try to stop us from up leveling. This is fueling that resistance. Recognize what it is and release it.

As you determine situations to apply your newly unlocked authentic leadership gifts you will want to ease into them, test how

---

[16] Rajesh, Anushka, "The Death of Workplace Hierarchy - Giving rise to a new organizational structure" *PeopleHum,* https://www.peoplehum.com/blog/the-death-of-hierarchy

others react and even minimize the impact or effect they are having on the team and situations. That's okay. Have you ever heard the phrase 'just rip off the band-aid'? Put yourself out there! Go all in! What can it possibly hurt?

Showing up as Nurturer to help provide support and empathy to team members struggling with overwhelm might look like helping them to re-prioritize work and parking lot some less important items to give them some breathing room.

Showing up as Visionary to provide a look into possibilities that have not been discovered or thought up yet to others to spark inspiration and drive innovation. This might look like pulling data, gathering feedback, and supporting ideation.

Showing up as Igniter to get things started. This might look like pushing others out of their comfort zone or perfectionist mindset to launch a new process or program.

Showing up as Advocate to genuinely acknowledge the efforts someone is making and how valuable they are to the team and customers can help them connect back into the mission.

Showing up as Multiplier and believing in others to unlock their skills and capacities that can have a significant and scalable impact.

Showing up as Clarifier to establish alignment around what is needed, strategy and expectations allowing others to drive forward in a way that feels like it clicks. This might also look like feedback in a direct way to ensure there is no ambiguity.

Showing up as Connector to offer yourself as a bridge to the big picture and others in a way that is genuine and meets others where they are. This might look like reaching out to a stakeholder organization to better understand how your team can support them more effectively.

Showing up as Enabler to identify what is needed to support an empowered culture. This might look like asking teams what training would help them make decisions they are expected to make or access to data or systems that would help them feel more confident.

Showing up as Champion to hit discomfort head on and support the team. This might look like being a change leader with feedback loops set up to ensure voices are heard as to be a champion to the people side of change.

Showing up as Collaborator to spark genuine co-creation with others in a way that does not have a preset agenda, force, or hierarchical structure. This might look like a cross-departmental collection of diverse backgrounds and thinking with an agreed upon outcome to solve for sharing equal responsibility for achieving that outcome.

Showing up as Reinforcer to hold space/container for the present to evaluate successes and failures in a way where learnings are established. This might also look like ensuring team members understand the value they bring to the team and company or customers.

Your authentic leadership gifts are the formula for success that will align with the evolved leadership needs as we head further into uncertainty and unpredictability together.

33

THE EVOLUTION

It takes courage to be yourself in a world where you are constantly told that who you are isn't enough. Being yourself is the biggest gift you can offer yourself and others. Be brave enough to show the world who you are without an apology
——Ash Alves on Authenticity

Summary

Authentic leadership is a collection of skills, gifts and capacities that are evolving and emerging. They are surfacing because they are needed and because we are ready to bring them forth in a new way of leading. As leaders can work through the blocks holding them in a place of outdated modals and as outdated models fade into the background authentic leadership will take root in powerful ways.

The impact leaders play in the future of business, community and the world are critical now more than ever. There is always a now that ignites the path to the future. It's about holding space for the continued evolution and expansion of those skills and capacities to take shape. We are not perfect humans or leaders. I believe the shift to being more human as an authentic leader is where more of these gifts will emerge.

Creating flow and fluidity in the uncertainty and unpredictability is how these gifts will influence future generations, speed up innovation towards solutions of our world's greatest problems and establish the most connection we have ever had as a society. All those feelings of more meaningful work, connection to self and others, serving others, expansion into your best self and a greater purpose are hitting us all now because we are ready, and we are needed.

Focus on how you can evolve your own leadership that is authentic to you and provides vulnerability to bring forth your gifts. The world needs you.

AFTERWORD

In my conversation with Linda, we spoke about how false ego can get in the way of authentic leadership. She suggested frequent 360s to measure how authentic leadership is taking hold across the team. She shares the importance of getting the temperature of how things are landing in the team versus how things are being managed up.

Linda believes it's important to champion authentic leadership while building development plans for those that lead from false ego. There are still many leaders who are driven by false ego and have made an art out of managing up while the people in their team are unhappy because they believe their leader cares about themselves more than the team.

It's important to make it super clear to people who lead from false ego what their development areas are and build a plan that leads them to authenticity. This can be hard, as there are some who will challenge the feedback and will deflect.

Senior leaders must have the fortitude to push forward with development regardless to build a high-performing team and a culture of trust through authenticity.

ACKNOWLEDGMENTS

I'm so grateful for the amazing people who spent time sharing their observations and experiences that contributed to this book. Raquel (Rach) Acuna, Michelle Curtis, Janee Francks, Jesse Gott, Sara Phillips, Deena Piquion, David Ponraj, Linda Rendleman, Nicko Roussos, and Stephen Tessitore. Their real-time feedback and perceptions of what is and isn't working in leadership was so impactful. I also appreciate allowing us to tap into their journeys and evolution in their leadership styles, skills, and capacities over time. They are a representation of our leaders of the future and each in their own way contribute to how we can show up fully in our authentic leadership.

Thank you, Lauren Diamond, for another great book cover and Shawna Benson for a fun photo shoot in Montana where we were able to capture the back cover photo.

I'd like to thank all the mentors, teachers, guides, and those who inspired me with their missions and work over the years. There are too many to name. I'd also like to acknowledge the many mentees who guided me as much as I guided them over the years. The leaders who modeled the future with their authentic gifts.

Thank you to my parents who created a safe space for my sisters and I to be our authentic selves, and who modeled many of the leadership gifts outlined in this book. What a great way to grow up!

Thank you to my love, partner, and best friend John. You have been amazing on this journey. Thank you for your support, love, and space to bring this to life. I love life with you.

Bibliography

Below is a list of books that has shaped my learning.

Haddock, Jack H., (2015). *The Subconscious Mind: How to Unlock the Powerful Force of Your Subconscious Mind*. Createspace Independent Publishing Platform.

Swart, Tara (MD, PhD), (2019). *The Source: The Secrets of the Universe, the Science of the Brain*. Harper One.

Bhat, Nilima: Sisodia, Raj, (2016). *Shakti Leadership: Embracing Feminine and Masculine Power in Business*. Berrett-Koehler Publisher.

Hendricks, Gay, (2009). *The Big Leap: Conquer Your Hidden Fear and Take Life to the Next Level*. Harper One.

Singer, Michael A., (2015). *The Surrender Experiment: my journey into life's perfection*. Harmony/Rodale.

Grant, Adam, (2021). *Think Again: The Power of Knowing What you Don't Know*. Diversified Publishing.

Gilbert, Elizabeth, (2015). *Big Magic: Creative Living Beyond Fear*. Riverhead Books.

Dweck, Carol S., (2006). *Mindset: The New Psychology of Success*. Random House.

McKeown, Greg, (2011). *Essentialism: The Disciplined Pursuit of Less*. Crown Business.

Bernstein, Gabrielle, (2018). *Judgment Detox: Release the Beliefs That Hold You Back from Living a better Life*. Gallery Books.

Chopra, Deepak, (2002). *Reinventing the Body, Resurrecting the Soul: How to Create a New You.* Harmony.

Bernstein, Gabrielle, (2019). *Super Attractor: Methods for Manifesting a Life Beyond Your Wildest Dreams.* Hay House.

Ambrosini, Melissa, (2016). *Mastering Your Mean Girl: The no BS guide to Silencing Your Inner Critic and becoming wildly Wealthy, fabulously Healthy and bursting with Love.* TarcherPerigee

Godin, Seth, (2008). *Tribes: We Need You to Lead Us.* Portfolio.

Robbins, Mel, (2017). *The 5 Second Rule: Transform Your Life, Work, and Confidence with Everyday Courage.* Savio Republic

Sincero, Jen, (2018). *You are a Badass Every Day: How to Keep Your Motivation Strong, Your Vibe High, and Your Quest for Transformation Unstoppable.* Penguin Life.

Hsieh, Tony, (2010). *Delivering Happiness: A Path to Profits, Passion and Purpose.* Grand Central Publishing.

Brown, Brene, (2008). *I Thought it was Just Me (but it isn't): Telling the Truth About Perfectionism, Inadequacy and power.* Gotham Books.

Sinek, Simon, (2014). *Leaders Eat Last.* Portfolio.

Sinek, Simon (2009). *Start With Why: How Great leaders Inspire Everyone To Take Action.* Portfolio.

Brown, Brene, (2015). *Rising Strong: How the Ability to Reset Transforms the Way We Live, Love, Parent, and Lead.* Spiegel & Grau.

Pressfield, Steven, (2002). *The War of Art: Winning The Inner Creative Battle.* Warner Books.

Granger, Jennifer, (2014). *Feminine Lost: Why Most Women are Male.* Hachette Books.

Kelley, Tom; Kelley, David, (2013). *Creative Confidence: Unleashing the Creative Potential Within Us All.* Crown Business.

There are so many other resources including Newsletters, online courses, and live courses I have learned so much from over the years.

Going Deeper

If you're new to Authentic Me Revolution, let me introduce myself! I'm Angie McCourt, author, coach, podcast host and app/course curator.

I've spent 27 years in the corporate world and dove into the coaching space at a time when people are looking to live purposeful.

The reason I wrote this book was to bring to light the evolution of leadership and all those struggles that keep us from showing up as an authentic leader. It's time to make the shift!

I want you to *BRIDGE THE GAP BETWEEN WHO + WHERE YOU ARE TO WHO + WHERE YOU WANT TO BE.*
I want you to *SHIFT YOUR MINDSET FROM LACK + LIMITATIONS TO SUCCESS + HAPPINESS*
I want you to *CREATE A VISION, STRATEGY AND PLAN TO ACHIEVE YOUR GOALS*
I want you to *BUILD AUTHENTIC, TRUSTING RELATIONSHPIS BY BEING YOUR TRUE AUTHENTIC SELF.*
I want you to *KICK THAT IMPOSTER SYNDROME AND SELF DOUBT IN THE BOOTY AND FEEL CONFIDENT.*
I want you to *ESTABLISH NEW HABITS THAT HELP YOU SUSTAIN A BALANCED SELF*

Check out my website www.angiemcourt.com/loveyourgifts where you can sign up for my Newsletter and access free resources.
Goodbye Imposter Syndrome 21-Day Challenge
Career Reboot online www.angiemccourt.com/career-reboot-intensive
Podcast – Shifting Inside Out on Spotify, Apple, Google, Audible

About the Author

Angie McCourt is an Author, Host of Shifting Inside Out podcast and Founder, App/course curator of Authentic Me Revolution. She backs her experience with a 27-year career as a successful business leader and coaching depth of skills and research at a time where major change can happen including revolutionizing the workplace and life in general. Her hope is to help others shift their limiting beliefs and discover their elevated gifts so they can show up as their best self and best leader.

She is a Connector, Clarifier and Multiplier discovered along her own journey of leadership evolution. She has challenged status quo leadership skills throughout her career and work in the community.

This is her second published book and has an App available in the App store and Google Play store called Best.Self.Activation focusing on personal transformation overcoming blocks and inner barriers.

Angie's mission is to help others discover their gifts, be true to their best self and unlock their authentic leadership potential.

Visit www.angiemccourt.com
Follow on Instagram @Angie_McCourt
Follow on LinkedIn @AngieBeltzMcCourt

www.ingramcontent.com/pod-product-compliance
Lightning Source LLC
Chambersburg PA
CBHW011958090526
44590CB00023B/3766